THE CIVILIZATION OF THE AMERICAN INDIAN

The Hopis:
PORTRAIT OF A DESERT PEOPLE

by *Walter Collins O'Kane*
with photographs in color by the author

University of Oklahoma Press
Norman

by WALTER COLLINS O'KANE

Injurious Insects (New York, 1913)
Jim and Peggy at Meadowbrook Farm (New York, 1917)
Jim and Peggy at Appletop Farm (New York, 1923)
Trails and Summits of the White Mountains (Boston, 1925)
Trails and Summits of the Green Mountains (Boston, 1926)
Trails and Summits of the Adirondacks (Boston, 1928)
Sun in the Sky (Norman, 1950)
The Hopis: Portrait of a Desert People (Norman, 1953)

Library of Congress Card Catalog 53–5477

Copyright 1953 by the University of Oklahoma Press
Publishing Division of the University. Composed and
printed at Norman, Oklahoma, U.S.A., by the University
of Oklahoma Press. First edition, March, 1953.
Second printing, March, 1954.

*To the valued Hopi friends who have welcomed me into
their homes, have permitted me to share in their beliefs
and experiences, have reviewed what I have written—and
who in their accustomed way would wish to remain unnamed*

FOREWORD

THE OLDEST LIVING GENERATION of the Hopis—they and their ways are the genesis of this book. Part of an ancient society, which has remained but little changed for many generations, they conform to the ways and beliefs of that society. They share together the views and the customs which they inherited from their ancestors. But each of them as an individual has been cast in his own mold. His characteristics conform to that mold. His features, his manner, are his own, and these do not change. He will be the same tomorrow, next month, next year, as he is today.

He and the rest of his generation have handed down to sons and grandsons the beliefs and ways which were transmitted from fathers and grandfathers. Those strong beliefs influence the younger generations deeply. But the world surrounding the Hopi people is not the same as it was a hundred years ago. Slowly but inexorably the altered contacts must make themselves felt; new influences must have their effect. The oldest generation represents in impressive degree the old values, the old Hopi way of life. That generation is made up now of men and women who are eighty years old, ninety, ninety-five. Inevitably they are passing.

In this book I wish to record some of their ways, and through the portraits to preserve the character which looks out upon the world from their eyes.

I am indebted to the John Simon Guggenheim Memorial Foundation for an award which made possible the engraving of the color plates in this book, and to my long-time friend, Otto Haas, for generous assistance in connection with the engraving.

The Journals of Alexander M. Stephen, through their editor, Elsie Clews Parsons, have been drawn on for many details of the winter solstice ceremony and for certain Hopi language relationships.

To my Hopi friend Nava'yoi yava I am indebted for painstaking review of several chapters of this book.

I wish also to acknowledge my debt to Alfred F. Whiting whose thorough monograph, *Ethnobotany of the Hopi,* published as Bulletin 15 of the Museum of Northern Arizona, provided many suggestions and essential verifications.

WALTER COLLINS O'KANE

Durham, New Hampshire
January 5, 1953

viii

THE CONTENTS

THE PORTRAITS

The Hopis:
PORTRAIT OF
A DESERT PEOPLE

LOOKING WITHIN

M ANY YEARS HAVE ELAPSED since I first began paying visits to the Hopi Indians of northern Arizona. In the course of these years it has become possible not only to witness many of the activities of these people but also to gain some understanding of the significance attached to that which I have witnessed and heard. Slowly the visitor in various homes has become the friend, and understanding has grown with the experience.

In any casual first visit in the Hopi reservation, that which you see is not likely to be rightly appraised. Everything of a material nature is different from that to which the white man is accustomed. The country is different, with its vast expanse of rock-strewn mesas, its rabbit brush and juniper, its naked can-yons, and its flood-scoured arroyos in which no water flows except after a cloudburst. The fields, the crops, the villages, the houses—all are different. The ceremony in a plaza is alien and mysterious and not in the least understood as to its true meaning. These are the outward aspects, and these are all that a casual visit is likely to disclose.

In such a visit the men and women whom you see will be absorbed in their own affairs, whether attending a ceremony which you also are witnessing, or going about their daily activities, carrying water, chopping wood, returning from the fields, or making purchases at a trading post. Being a reserved people they will not have much to say to you, although most of them speak English. Usually the children seem not to be particularly interested in the white stranger. They also have their own accustomed activities.

Little by little, if you pay further visits, as do some of the whites who live in Arizona or California, you begin to understand why most of the villages are laid out around a plaza, with adjacent streets running helter-skelter, why the houses are built of stone and have a flat, earth-covered roof, why the fields are irregular, the corn planted in widely spaced, many stalked hills, why the springs continue to be the jealously guarded sources of water, why the Hopi storekeeper almost indignantly refuses to sell you a crude little prehistoric pitcher that was found in some near-by ruin. Watching the faces of the men and women who are attending a ceremony, considering the long tradition that lies behind each detail of costume, each word in a chant, each sequence of notes, realizing the completeness of participation that each actor shares—here you feel a dawning comprehension of the drama and the prayers which it embodies.

When the visitor has been accepted as a friend in a Hopi home, the feeling of understanding again increases. In the conversations and in the silences, some of your formless questions are answered. That indeed is the only way in which real enlightenment on matters of vital import is likely to come. If you set about asking questions, one after another, you will meet with quiet courtesy but also an unmistakable reserve. Why should your host or hostess be catechised by you? Would you wish to have the same experience from a visitor in your home? Perhaps you would not be unwilling, but a Hopi is a person of inflexible independence. His life is completely his own, and his home is held by him and by other Hopis as a place inviolate.

Beneath it all you will realize, sooner or later, that, no matter how good a friend you may be considered, no matter how cordially you may be welcomed, no matter how sincere may be the greetings when you arrive for a visit, you still are a member of the white race. All of the attitudes and acts of the whites toward the Hopis for the last hundred years have created a setting which you cannot quite wholly escape. It is not a conscious or spoken reservation on the part of your Hopi friend. Perhaps it may not be realized. But in actuality it is there, and unavoidably it has its influence, subtle but real. Ever since the white race made contact with the Hopis it has brought pressure to bear upon them. Some of this was necessary because the two must live together, which means that somehow the smaller must adapt itself to the larger. But with some exceptions the seriously harmful and upsetting element has been the spirit in which the whites have approached the Hopis. To be looked upon as inferior, to be told that better ways are in store for you—this is the corroding factor whose scars never quite disappear and whose influence is bound sometimes to be felt.

The Hopis are a proud people, and justly so. They need only understanding, not apology. In an environment which no white man would find adequate or tolerable they have been self-supporting and self-sufficient. They have maintained their ancient crafts and arts, and have upheld personal independence. For many generations they have educated their boys and girls in those matters which would make them well-trained men and women, able to establish homes of their own. They have adhered to a belief in peace, and in well-wishing toward all other human beings.

5

The Hopis

They have not been faultless. Their rigidity of opinion has led them sometimes to a fixed attitude which, though wrong, was inflexible. Their absorption with a spirit world has resulted at times in self-induced fears and harmful concepts. In their compact and closely knit villages, factions have developed on occasion, and quarrels, bitter though bloodless, have resulted. Here and there an individual, too ready with suspicion, has turned against others who were entitled to be his friends. After all they are human beings with human faults and weaknesses. Nevertheless, they are a remarkable people.

In *Sun in the Sky* I endeavored to convey to the reader some idea of the Hopi country, their villages and agriculture, their homes and home life, their traditions and ceremonies. In this new book I wish to go further and to illuminate, as much as I can, Hopi ways and beliefs, especially those of the older generations. Often the beliefs must be formulated from the ways; the Hopis are not given to setting forth doctrines or principles of conduct. Although a belief may be firmly held, it is likely to be so tacitly accepted that it does not take the form of explicit statement; yet it may be the universal basis of thought and judgment. As such, it makes itself evident through the way in which the people conduct their lives, through their daily activities, their attitudes toward those activities, their reactions to the problems of living, their acceptance or rejection of the views and expedients suggested by human existence.

The men and women who have taken part in the incidents and experiences related here have been given Hopi names which are other than their own. This has been done because a Hopi does not wish to be set up as one who has accomplished certain achievements or has had certain experiences. To be singled out is contrary to his training and desires.

6

Looking Within

Since the old Hopi ways are the foundation of Hopi character, and since character is expressed in the features, especially among those who are advanced in years, the illustrations in this book are portraits of representative Hopis. All of the portraits are engravings from photographs in color which I have been making the last two or three years. Some of the subjects had never before been photographed. It has been possible to include them only because of the help and intercession of Hopi friends.

In these faces I find a poise, a steadfast outlook on the world, which seems to me the embodiment of all that is best in the old Hopi way of life. These people have had few of the material advantages which the white man has brought into existence, the complex inventions of Western civilization. No electricity brings to their homes the conveniences which we enjoy and which, for us, have become necessities rather than luxuries. Of all the manifold things that are set before us in store windows and in the pages of our magazines they possess almost none. Their contentment and self-sufficiency are not based on possession of things but rather on something else which is intangible and which to them is important and rewarding. Perhaps what they have is not without significance.

THE ANCIENT PATTERN

A HOPI HOUSEHOLD is a self-directing group, the members of which seem to achieve an automatic co-ordination of their activities. No one tells the others what they should do, or when, or how. No one exercises authority. The various members seem to fall naturally into a pattern in which the abilities of the individual and the needs of the household are satisfactorily served, a pattern which probably was evolved so long ago that it requires no direction and is accepted without question.

To a visitor, a household seldom, if ever, gives the impression of being in a hurry or working under pressure. It does not time its duties by a clock. Indeed a clock is not likely to be anywhere in evidence, and I doubt if most households own one, or keep it wound if they do. The family does not usually operate on the basis of duties or appointments which must be fulfilled at a certain hour. The members are likely to sit down to a meal when the food is ready or when they so desire, not when a specific hour has arrived. Breakfast may be quite early if there are crops needing attention, or it may be quite late if that is desirable. In the summer months, the evening meal may be eaten outdoors after darkness has come and the bright stars illuminate the desert sky. In winter, bedtime may come early because not much can be done in weaving or basketry or other crafts in darkness or by the light of an oil lamp. The sun has much to do with home activities.

In winter or summer, there is little likelihood that anyone will desire to sit up late in order to look at a newspaper or listen to a radio. Newspapers are seldom found in a Hopi home. They offer little that is of interest in comparison with affairs nearer at hand. The world of the cities, with which newspapers are naturally concerned, is a long way from the Hopi world. The realm of new and complex inventions is interesting but not vital. The devastating events on other continents, the wars and prospects of wars, the complexities of conflicting civilizations, are alien. Being terrible and destructive, they should not be thought about too much. As for radios, an occasional Hopi home possesses one, but they are rare. Since they are battery powered, and since the battery is probably run down and is not important enough to be renewed, a radio program, whether news or something else, seldom is heard.

To a Hopi, the affairs of his own household and those of his neighbors and his village, the raising and harvesting of crops, the practice of traditional crafts, the preparation for ceremonies and participation in them, the visits to and from relatives—these are the matters which command interest. They are close at hand, understandable, and constructive; they are worth thinking about.

I have been acquainted with Kwa'taka for a year or two but had never met his wife Ka'chi, although I knew her by sight and knew in what part of the village their home is situated. I also knew that, according to ancient custom, a Hopi house belongs to the wife, not the husband. Approaching a group of houses one day, I saw Ka'chi stepping out of a doorway. I stopped. "This must be Kwa'taka's house," I said. Ka'chi smiled but promptly replied, "Oh no! This isn't Kwa'taka's house. He just lives here."

Sitting in her home I watched the activities that were proceeding—the characteristic life of an old-time Hopi household. Ka'chi was seated on a mat on the floor, finishing the last coils of a basket. It was an attractive specimen, its design interesting, its colors soft and pleasing. Ka'chi worked with a sure touch, thrusting the awl through a coil at just the right angle to maintain the symmetry of the basket, drawing the yucca binder smoothly tight. She was unhurried and manifestly enjoyed her work. A ten-year-old granddaughter, seated beside her, was learning the craft and finding that it required practice and experience. The small disk which she was making, intended to be the flat base of a plaque or basket, was acquiring a warped contour which would not serve. For her, the awl thrust was not yet quite what it should be, but she also was patient and unhurried. The next one would turn out better.

A daughter knelt behind one of the metates, the one with the finer grain, and proceeded with the final grinding of the heap of blue cornmeal waiting at its base. Deftly she swept part of the meal onto the stone with her slender brush of hairgrass and ground it with the stone mano held in her two hands. Later the meal would be used in making piki, for tomorrow would be the final day of the *Niman* ceremony and a supply of piki would be needed. Relatives would be arriving from another village and would be visiting the household. Ka'chi got up from her mat and left to start a small fire, a very small fire at first, under the smooth stone on which the piki would be made. The stone must be warmed up slowly, a little at a time.

Kwa'taka came in, poured water into a basin, removed the bright bandeau that bound his hair, and washed his face and neck, his hands and arms. He was building an addition to the house, an enlargement rather, since it was not to be an extra room. I went out with him to look at the work that he had been doing. The stone wall, running around three sides of the selected space, was about two feet high. He had started it several weeks before but was not trying to complete it on any set schedule. When there was suitable opportunity he prepared sand and clay mortar and laid up some more stones. He explained his plan to me.

"When I have it as high as the house," he said, "I'll put on the roof and take out the wall where this joins the house. That way I'll make the room in there a big one. Then when other members of our family come to see us, when there is a ceremony, we can have many all together in the house."

Kwa'taka's house has only two rooms. With the addition it would still have only two. But there would be more fun in having a big room than in possessing a third.

When we came back into the house, I noted that some one had removed the white cloth that covered a dozen round loaves of bread arrayed on the table. They looked invitingly brown and crusty. I knew that they had been baked in an outdoor oven and that they had been made in preparation for the *Niman*. The guests and relatives would expect this bread and find special enjoyment in it, just as they would count on mutton stew and piki, and would expect the food to be placed on a mat on the floor, around which they would gather on other mats.

Ka'chi had disappeared, presumably to maintain the slow fire under the piki stone. The daughter was making ready a vessel of boiling hot water with which to make batter for the piki. The ten-year-old granddaughter had started a new base for a coiled basket and was working at it thoughtfully, estimating with care the proper angle for the awl. Presently there was a

II

NA'MOKI

He is in his late eighties, and he is one of the influential
men of First Mesa. His name means "Medicine pouch"
and is pronounced Nah'-moh-kee. He is the husband
of Len'mana and shares with her a home near the tip
of Walpi, adjacent to the Chief Kiva.

knock on the door. Kwa'taka called to the visitor to enter, using an ancient Hopi phrase which in a mystic way means more than just "Come in!"

The man who appeared through the door and quietly accepted the low stool that was provided for him was somewhat older than Kwa'taka but had the same steadfast, untroubled look and the same well-poised, unhurried way. He did not immediately say anything, nor did Kwa'taka. Presently the two men began talking together in an animated manner, but I noted, as I had many times before, that, when one was speaking, the other remained silent until the first had finished, except perhaps to assent now and then with a single *"Aui,"* "Yes." What they were talking about was beyond my ken, since their conversation was in Hopi.

After a while the visitor untied the knots of a handkerchief which he was carrying and disclosed three or four bracelets, half a dozen rings, and a necklace, all set with turquoise. The men examined these, one by one, and presumably exchanged comment on the workmanship of the silver and the character of the settings. Kwa'taka turned to me. "He's going to take these to the big meeting at Gallup," he explained. "He wants me to go with him and bring along a blanket that I am thinking of selling. That's a good place to sell things. Lots of people there." He went to a chest that stood against a wall and brought back the blanket, a handsome one, woven in widely spaced gray and black bars that crossed to form darker gray blocks. Apparently they agreed on the price that it should bring for I caught the words "eighty dollars" and the evidence of agreement in their manner. I saw too that they repeatedly examined the necklace, which both admired.

"We've gone on trips before," Kwa'taka said. "If somebody

wants something that one of us hasn't got, maybe the other one has it and can make a good trade."

I have seen two old Hopi friends engaged in a similar enterprise, each of them with a folded blanket over a shoulder, each wearing a necklace, each with additional silver and turquoise tied in a handkerchief and stowed securely in a pocket. They were having a good time. In fact, they were like two boys on a holiday, and they were finding customers.

A sound outside caught my attention. It was like the clop, clop, of a burro, but the sound appeared hollow and as if made by tin or sheet iron. I excused myself and went outside to have a look. The "burro," I found, was a small boy moving along at a brisk pace on all fours. In each hand he held an empty tin can. These extended his arms sufficiently to permit fast progress while at the same time producing a satisfactory sound. A still smaller boy was riding on the back of the "burro," his legs clasping his mount tightly. In his hand he carried a two-foot length of string which served as an adequate imitation of a whip. Like the men with the blankets and jewelry they were having a good time.

A Hopi boy has few mechanical toys to get out of order; certainly, no mechanical trains. A tin-can burro is more realistic, costs nothing to acquire, and, like a burro himself, is economical in upkeep.

From near the outskirts of the village, I heard children's voices singing lustily. They came from the direction of a trail which leads to a spring. In a few moments the children appeared. Two small girls were riding on a burro which carried also a five-gallon can of water on each side, fastened on a framework like a sort of packsaddle. The proprietor walked along in the rear. As long as I could see the procession, and afterwards, the vigorous concert continued. Presumably, getting water would be a chore—at least it would be to most of us—but in this case it was also an adventure. I think that the man walking behind, and even the burro, must have derived something from the spirit of the lively accompaniment.

In another part of the village I discovered another concert. This one came from the interior of a homemade shelter in the open space back of a house. A framework, which may have been discarded from the body of a truck, had been covered sketchily with odds and ends of old blankets and canvas. Inside there must have been four or five youngsters. Without any intervals of silence or talking, they were maintaining a continuous round of enthusiastic singing while one of them accented the rhythm with vigorous whacks on some object that represented the drum used by their elders in a ceremony. For a while they would do one of the songs which are a part of a ceremony and which are unlike anything in our experience or anything that we could repeat if we desired. Then they would switch to one or another of our own familiar songs, current or dating back many years, learned probably in school. With vigor and enthusiasm and without a break, they would switch back again to something from the Hopi world. They were still at it when I left to visit my elderly friends who lived close by, Tu'va and his wife, Hon'mana.

Tu'va is a soft-spoken Hopi whose clear eyes and erect bearing belie his eighty-odd years. Hon'mana is equally quiet and unassuming but not so erect. Like many other Hopi women, she has long since taken on weight, although her strength and endurance seem unimpaired. Their home is one of the older ones of the village, built a hundred or more years ago and now only a little changed. Its two rooms are small. Its windows look out upon a village street where many generations of children have played and grown up together. In the living room, bunches of roasted

17

and dried ears of sweet corn hang along the top of a wall. In the winter, two walls are so occupied. Now only a few bunches remained, since the new crop was not yet ready. Here and there a downy feather from an eagle depended from a short cotton string fastened to a small stick that was thrust into the closely-packed brush over a ceiling beam—gifts from the winter solstice ceremony to signify a blessing on the house and its occupants. A coiled plaque, made by Hon'mana, decorated one of the walls. Two Kachina dolls, made by Tu'va, gave a gay note to another. Although these two Hopis are no longer young, they have not forgotten their crafts.

The storeroom which is an adjunct of their house is more than half as large as the dwelling. It is their insurance against a possible year of privation, their alternate for some of the public measures which have come into being in our white man's world. Its value is reflected in their attitude of confidence, their self-sufficiency. Tu'va took me into the storeroom, and although a new harvest season would soon be at hand, it was even now well stocked. Ears of corn, sorted by color, were neatly corded— enough to carry them through and beyond a whole year of crop failure. Some of the corn was two or three years old. Bags of shelled beans, pieces of dried mutton strung on a wire, bunches of dried string beans, vines, pods and all—the supplies on hand were varied and plentiful. Later there would be watermelons available until January, and squashes throughout the winter.

I noticed two items that I had not seen before elsewhere. Curious dried spirals hung from three or four nails. These, I learned, were prepared from a young squash by removing the rind and cutting the meat in a long spiral, which was hung up in the bright sun to dry. "But you must use a young squash, not an old one," Tu'va cautioned. On another nail there was a big crook-neck gourd which was hollow and had a round opening in the shell where the stem began to enlarge to form the round body. It looked like something intended for nesting birds, but Tu'va set me right. "We used to have those for carrying water," he explained. "You carried it by the crook over your shoulder. When you made one you first cut the hole, then cooked the gourd, and then cleaned out the inside."

Tu'va and Hon'mana have retained some of the old Hopi ways which others, especially the younger generations, no longer follow—customs which have no compelling significance and therefore yield to more convenient ways. Although there is a table in their living room, they usually prefer to eat from a mat placed on the floor. They sit before this on other mats, preserving the postures which tradition has established. Hon'mana sits squarely, as though she had first kneeled and then sat back with her legs doubled beneath her. Tu'va sits with his left leg doubled under him, the right leg with knee elevated and foot squarely on the floor, a little advanced. "That is the way a man must sit," he explained to me. "Then if anything happens and he needs to protect his family he can spring up quickly." If a girl or a young unmarried woman is present, I was told, she sits on both hips but with her legs at one side, doubled at the knee and drawn in closely. In that way her skirt covers her legs down to her feet.

I noticed on the table a heap of watermelon seeds piled up on a small tray. Hon'mana followed my eyes. "That's to use with hominy," she said. "First you roast them. Then you grind them up. Then you soak them in hot water. And then you pour the liquid over the hominy. That makes the hominy taste good."

Tu'va corroborated. "It tastes fine," he said.

"Is this for the ceremony tomorrow?" I asked Hon'mana.

"Oh no. We have it as long as we have any watermelon seeds."

19

"There's one thing though," she added, "that we'll have just tomorrow. Just at time of a ceremony. We make a gravy of cornmeal and water. No meat in it. No salt. If we used any salt or meat, it wouldn't be right. We use that on *pi'kalup kuto'ki.* You know what that is? It's crumbled piki."

"And *pi'kami,* too," Tu'va suggested

"Yes, we have that in the morning before a ceremony. We make it with cornmeal and sprouted grain. We make these into a pudding and steam it."

Two small bows leaned against a wall, awaiting decorations. Tu'va had made these out of juniper branches. They were not large enough or strong enough to serve as hunting bows, but were intended as gifts to be presented at the *Niman* ceremony the next day. As such, they would symbolize more than mere toys and would eventually find their place on living-room walls. The arrows to go with them needed feathering. For this Tu'va had an eagle pinion ready, a straight and strong feather which would suffice for three or four arrows. These and the bows would receive their final touches before sundown.

The house occupied by Dan and Elsie Humi'ta, situated a few minutes walk from that of Tu'va and Hon'mana, is different in some ways but is typical of many to be found today in the Hopi villages, especially the houses erected in the last thirty or forty years. Though built of stone and though it has only two rooms, its living room is larger, its walls and ceiling are plastered, and its floors are made of matched boards. Also its windows are larger, and there are more of them. There are more cooking utensils, a larger stove, a kitchen cabinet, and more dishes on which to serve food, as well as more chairs to place before the table at mealtime. These are the material aspects, reflecting a desire for

The Ancient Pattern

greater comfort. In other respects the home activities and especially the home attitude and atmosphere are but little changed.

Dan and Elsie are in their fifties. Both received part of their education beyond the borders of the reservation, as have many other Hopis who represent their generation. Elsie uses her husband's name together with the white name which was given her when she was a baby. This has no important significance; it is merely a convenience, since it accords with white custom. She has her own Hopi name but seldom has occasion to use it. She dresses as white women do, is ordinarily sparing of turquoise jewelry, but owns a handsome necklace and rings which are worn on occasion—as indeed a woman of our own race would do. Her household activities are essentially the same as those of other Hopi women. Like them, she sometimes grinds corn on a metate and makes piki on the traditional polished stone. She is skilled in basketry and follows her craft consistently.

If you did not know Dan and were to meet him at the trading post or in Winslow, you might think of him as one who lives in town. He wears the same clothes that we wear. His hair is dressed like ours. He wears no turquoise in his ears and no jewelry other than a single ring. This of course is on an ordinary everyday occasion. Actually he owns two or three elaborate and valuable necklaces, which he sometimes wears, for he participates in more than one of the ancient ceremonies and attends others. The manner of dressing his hair is not viewed as of consequence. The bob and the bright bandeau are not fixed by ancient tradition and have no vital significance.

In daily activities, Dan's life is typical. He has his crops to attend to, and these occupy much of his time during the growing and harvest seasons. He takes his turn at herding sheep. He owns a truck which he uses for various activities, including some which

LEN'MANA

Her name is pronounced Len'-mah-nah, and it means
"Flute maiden." She and her husband, Na'moki, live
in Walpi, at the very tip of First Mesa. To reach the
door of their home you climb stone steps, passing the
hatchway of the Chief Kiva. A squared roof beam within the house came from the prehistoric Walpi, which
was situated on a shelf below the top of First Mesa.
Len'mana was born in this same house. A note in the
journal of Alexander Stephen, written in December,
1892, speaks of a party then in progress celebrating
Len'mana's marriage.

add to his income. With his truck he hauls the water needed at home. He is interested in various matters of tribal welfare and problems and therefore has frequent contacts with the Indian Service and with the white man's views and regulations. In this he takes an active part, but always as an intelligent, keen-minded Hopi, not as one who has changed into the likeness of another race.

If you were to visit Dan and Elsie in their home, you would be impressed at the start by its appearance—the long and wide living room, the broad windows, the comfortable chairs, the painting of a Kachina dancer on the wall—but you would soon be equally impressed by the unchanged attitude, the unaltered characteristics of independence and self-sufficiency, and the absence of hurry and pressure. You would have found this same unchanged way of life when you came to the door and knocked —you do not just walk into a Hopi home, no matter who you are, Hopi or white, young or old, high or low. You first knock. In a real sense, a Hopi home is a private world and is not to be invaded at will. When you have knocked you are bidden to enter, and then, no matter who you may be, a chair is provided for you.

The house occupied by Dan and Elsie shows some change, but their home, reflecting their thoughts and beliefs, still has its foundations in the old Hopi way, still nourishes and protects the Hopi manner of life and principles of conduct. In spirit, nothing is altered.

WHATEVER YOU CAN DO

No matter what your age may be, no matter how old you are, you will always continue to do whatever you are able to do.

This philosophy is set forth in no precept or admonition among the Hopi people. No one has ever formulated it in words or, perhaps, has ever given it explicit thought. Born long ago out of necessity, continued through the centuries in a society that has been but little touched by a mechanistic age, a society in which each man is his own master and in which there is no laboring class working for hire and counting the hours, the custom has been as fixed as the revolution of the earth. A Hopi's physical fitness determines the nature and extent of his activity, his age has no bearing on the matter. This is the ancient Hopi way.

Consider Johnny.

I first saw Johnny when he was on his way to the spring. Three or four paths, which originate in various parts of the village, converge for a few steps in order to pass around a certain house before continuing their independent courses. The spot is a crossroad where you may meet almost anyone.

Johnny's Hopi name is Hon'hoya, which means Little Bear, but long ago some one called him Johnny, and everyone uses that name. He was approaching now on one of the paths. Although he

26

carried a staff he set it down vigorously, not as one who needed its support. Wiry and somewhat stooped, he walked with a springy step, as if the job in hand were an adventure, familiar but nevertheless one of potential interest. Under his chin were knotted the ends of a quilt which served as the means for carrying a burden on his back.

At the corner of the house he paused to exchange greetings with the owner, a Hopi matron whom I have known for several years. I perceived then that he was an old man, perhaps very old indeed. Short in stature, even for a Hopi, which means many inches less than our own, he was slender and seemed not to have an ounce of extra weight anywhere. His face was brown leather, as brown as an old saddle. His straight hair, falling almost to his shoulders and worn without the usual bright bandeau, was almost white. When my Hopi friend spoke to him she held her lips close to his ear and raised her voice to its maximum volume. That he really heard what she said seemed doubtful, but if not, his failure made no difference in his responsive manner. Although it turned out that he could not see very well, he gave no indication of the handicap. His eyes had the eager gleam of one who finds the surrounding world rewarding, however dim.

I felt of the pack on his back to learn what it might contain. The outlines of the object within were unmistakable—an empty five-gallon can. Johnny was on his way to fill the can at the spring, a half mile away, and to carry it back to his home.

The path that he was to follow leads across the broad, flat ledges of the top of the mesa. In occasional crevices an isolated red Indian paintbrush can be seen. In others, a prickly-pear cactus lies in wait with its spines. In some places the smooth rock is covered with patches of lichen, bluish gray in the dry desert air. At one point the trail crosses a broad, shallow depression, bor-

27

dered at its lower margin by a few square yards of soil, held in place by a low stone wall, followed by other small areas similarly contrived. Here, if rain falls, moisture can be retained and beans can be raised. Step by step, the path slowly loses altitude, and, if you look back, you discover that the houses of the village have disappeared over the rim of the world. On your right, across a great gulf, a distant prong of the mesa cuts across the sky line.

Suddenly the trail dives down a rocky gully where a few stones have been moved into position to give some sort of footing. The descent here is steep, and so is the climb when you return with your burden. Below this the path winds among big fragments of the mesa's face which have broken off and have lodged in confusion. A hundred feet beyond lies the spring, a broad pool, unprepossessing in the white man's view but serving the village for nearly three hundred years, and supplying the same community in its earlier site for several hundred more.

Over this path Johnny has carried water all his long life, perhaps for eighty years, perhaps more. He has not had the luxury of a burro that can carry two five-gallon cans instead of one, following a longer but easier route. Seemingly, Johnny has not cared to bother with a burro. Still less has he heeded the plan of the occasional Hopi householder who uses a pickup truck to bring water in a fifty-gallon drum from a storage tank several miles away where a windmill does the pumping. Week after week, year after year, Johnny has carried his supply on his own back, forty-five pounds, up the steep trail and across the mesa.

He still does just that.

On the farther side of the village, a hundred yards beyond the last row of dwellings, the mesa falls away in great vertical cliffs. At one place enormous fragments as big as a house have been dislodged and lie one upon another in giant confusion. The story goes that this disruption took place within the memory of the old folk and was understandably terrifying. In the midst of the precipitous array, a path on which burros can travel makes its way down to the vast country below. At another place, a trail which only human beings can follow leads down to another part of the area.

Standing on the mesa rim, you look down on a region that seems merely rolling but is actually made up of ridges and valleys, sandy plains and bordering hills. Small, irregular fields are scattered in the midst of these. Where sand has accumulated in slopes and dunes, peach trees are growing, their roots far down in soil protected from drouth by the overlying sand cover, which also lies ready to drink up and hold whatever rain may fall. Paths thread their way through all this, along with occasional wagon tracks, for, by a roundabout route, you can reach the region with a team of mules or a pickup truck. Still farther away, three or four miles distant, lie other fields where there is moisture beneath the surface of the ground.

Down there below the mesa, along with others of his village, Johnny has had his crop land, available for his use through the workings of the clan allotment system. With the first warm weather of spring he would descend one of the steep trails, carrying on his shoulder the ancient Hopi version of a hoe, a formidable, handmade implement with a blade as broad as your two hands and weighing many pounds. Week by week, as the season moved along, the trip was made. He often went daily, for there was much to do: preparation of the ground, planting, cultivation, more planting, more cultivation—corn, beans, melons, squashes; erection of little brush windbreaks to keep the young plants from being covered by sand and smothered, removal of windblown sand from those which were buried in spite of brush. Down the

29

trail in the early morning, when the eastern horizon begins to glow with the first light of dawn; back to the top of the mesa when the sun has entered the house of night and is about to close the door. This was continued while the crops were making their start, until finally they were safely established. Only then could Johnny spend a day now and then attending a ceremony or visiting other villages.

With the coming of harvest, more trips were made from the mesa rim to the fields down below. Loads of corn, squashes, and melons, to be stored away against the needs of fall and winter, were carried on his back. Just wiry human legs, a strong back, and an equally strong and wiry intent were all that he had. There was not even a burro.

This was Johnny's life for seventy or eighty years, until the last few seasons.

Now Johnny is raising his crops, his garden stuff, and whatever else he can contrive, on land that lies two miles or more from the village, but on top of the mesa instead of below its rim. Small plots are available out there which you can see as you drive along the road. They are not numerous, nor are they continuous. Some of the region is too sandy and dry. The soil over the bedrock of the mesa is very thin but crops can be grown, and out there Johnny has his "fields."

Within the limits of strength and the diminished resources of his faculties, he continues to raise his own food.

Beyond the small plots that lie on the tableland of the mesa, still another mile or two from the village, a trail descends into the upper part of a broad canyon. It leads to a resource that the village has used for uncounted decades — an outcropping of coal. In part, the layer of earth overlying the vein has been weathered away, in part it must be removed by shoveling.

Whatever You Can Do

All of the hundreds of square miles of the vast Black Mesa, the geologists say, is underlaid with coal — millions of tons. Some of it, in certain geologic strata, is of high quality. Where the mesa breaks down along its southerly margin, a vein may be exposed. That these outcrops have long been utilized by the Hopi people, even in prehistoric times, is revealed by ancient heaps of ash and debris. Indeed, there is evidence that coal was used for heating primitive homes before such use was adopted in Europe.

The vein of coal that lies a few miles from Johnny's village is of only fair quality; it is not as solid and clear as a deposit that cuts across a wash like a dike and serves another village to the west. But it is a convenient source of fuel. Some of the householders use burros to bring it to their homes; others drive trucks to a point close to the deposit or pass it by for another source of better coal farther away. For his own use, Johnny has found the fuel satisfactory, and he has elected to carry it on his back. Fifty pounds at a trip! one fortieth of a ton! — not a large amount when we think of coal in terms of multiple tons! But a backload, fed judiciously into the small stove in Johnny's compact quarters, can provide comfort for a surprising length of time. Tight stone walls and a low ceiling conserve warmth. Other houses, built in a solid row not many feet distant, serve as a barrier to the searching winter winds.

Water supply, food, fuel—these have been Johnny's contribution to his essentials of living. Today, at ninety or more, he finds his contribution, as much of it as he can manage, no less acceptable.

Whether you are a young Hopi of thirty or forty, or an older man of sixty or eighty, if you are not crippled or blind, your daily

31

MAHO

Born about eighty-eight years ago, Maho is one of the leaders on First Mesa. His name means "A small club," and is pronounced Mah'-hoh. His farming operations, including those of his son, are extensive. In some of the ancient ceremonies he has a significant part. All his life he has favored wearing a Navajo style felt hat with a tall crown and a straight brim. He suggested wearing it in this picture but agreed to adhere to the Hopi custom of not wearing a hat.

activities run along as always. You raise the crops that you need, you herd whatever sheep you possess, or you share jointly with others the care of a flock. You hitch up your team and make a round trip of eighty miles to secure wood for fuel. If you desire an addition on your house you secure the materials and build it. When duties slacken and there is opportunity, you work at your craft. When a ceremony is scheduled, you take time off to attend. All this means that your days are full but not crowded.

Out in front of his house, Mo'vi was saddling his burro. I do not know Mo'vi's exact age, but I am sure that three or four other men in the village are somewhere in the neighborhood of eighty and Mo'vi is older than they. The saddle had once belonged to the United States Army and was purchased thirty or forty years ago. Its leather cover was worn completely away. Long ago the cinches were replaced, probably more than once. They needed another renewal. The webbing was still fairly usable, but the thongs had given way, and pieces of rope, well frayed, had been substituted. When the saddle was fastened securely on the burro, or as nearly so as could be expected, Mo'vi spread an old coat over it to cover the bare frame. Around the burro's neck he loosely tied a strip of worn cotton cloth. Later this would be useful in hobbling his mount. Beside the door stood a hoe with a homemade handle of native shape and origin. With it was a straight stick, three feet long, to be used in guiding and persuading the burro.

Mounted in the saddle, with the old coat adjusted beneath him, the hoe across his lap, and the stick in his right hand, Mo'vi rode briskly away. In the Hopi country, a good burro, sleepy and slow as it may appear to be, is capable of surprisingly nimble movement when directed by an owner who has a full schedule.

35

The Hopis

Ahead lay a trip of four miles that took him down from the mesa to the country six hundred feet below and out across the desert to fields lying near a wash, where moisture beneath the dry surface enabled crops to grow. The corn there needed cultivation, and weeds had started to grow in the midst of the melons.

Sundown would find Mo'vi starting his return journey, up-hill this time and slower, a long day ended, but in Mo'vi's world a day satisfying in its accomplishments. His age of eighty years or more had nothing to do with the matter.

When I called at the home of my friend Taku'ri one evening his daughter said that he had not yet returned from his fields. When he might return she could not say. He had spoken of attending to a duty which, once started, would take a considerable time to complete and should not be interrupted in the middle. Since it would soon be night, with only a three-quarter moon to light the way, since I could not be certain in which field he might be working, and since the matter I wished to talk with him about could wait, I left for my quarters.

In the morning I came back. Taku'ri was eating his breakfast, which, as it developed, served also as his evening meal of the night before. He apologized for his absence the previous evening.

"I had a little work to do," he explained, "and didn't get it finished until about one o'clock this morning."

Taku'ri is not one of the oldest of Hopi men. Two years must pass before he will be eighty.

Twice we had called at Hona'spi's home, my Hopi friend and I, but each time he was away and probably would not be back until late. As we came within sight of the house, my companion would say, "No! He isn't home. His burro isn't there."

Whatever You Can Do

And it would prove to be true. The third time we had better luck and found him in, the burro tethered near by.

Hona'psi had been absent because he was taking his turn at herding sheep. Two other men, each with a small flock like his own, had joined forces with him. Each herded for three days, with a six-day interval for other duties, including the care of crops. The day that we found him at home, Hona'spi had finished hoeing his beans by early afternoon and was making a pair of moccasins. Herding would be resumed the next day and the long trip on his burro would again be made.

The season was one of prolonged and severe drouth. No rain of consequence had fallen for more than six months, and very little had fallen in an equal period before that. Pastures within reasonable distance of Hona'psi's village were dry and brown, if not exhausted. Care of the sheep meant getting up long before dawn, riding many miles across the desert to a temporary corral, staying with the flock throughout the day as they drifted and grazed, seeing them safely back into the corral at sundown, and returning in the dark, while the young moon sank below the mysterious rim of the world, the tang of the desert drifted through the air, and the sharp click-click of the burro's feet punctuated the slow creak of the saddle. Three days of this; then a shift to other duties.

"Why does he continue to keep sheep?" I asked my Hopi friend. The answer to this and my following questions indicated some wonder at my inquiry. He had always kept a flock. He needed the wool for his weaving, mutton for food, and pelts to use in trade. With pelts to barter, he had acquired the buckskin which he was using to make the pair of moccasins. The moccasins, in turn, would bring about fifteen dollars in cash, and that money would buy a half pound of rough turquoise.

37

The Hopis

"But how about the long trips on a burro and the prolonged days at herding?"

To this my friend answered "Why not? He has a good burro."

"How old is Hona′psi?" I asked.

"Oh, he's not old! About the same as I am."

My friend is eighty-five.

Nearly a year had elapsed since I had visited Du′wa's home. He lives in a remote corner of his village, and you do not catch sight of his house until you round a neighboring dwelling. When I returned a surprise awaited me. An addition had been built, a sizable room.

Du′wa has no small children in his household. In fact there are only two persons besides himself, both of them elderly. Apparently he had simply decided to have another room, and had proceeded to build it.

The stone for the walls he had obtained from a neighbor who quarries rough blocks from a near-by deposit. The smooth round rafters had been hauled from a place eighty miles away, also the frames for the windows and doors, and the sash and doors themselves.

A skillful stone mason, as most Hopis are, he had shaped his blocks and laid them up in the clay-and-sand mortar that he had learned to mix as a boy. The rafters, which were large and strong but not heavy, he had hoisted into position without much difficulty. The waterproof layer on top and the brush-and-earth roof came from the near-by land. The smooth, hard clay floor was now covered with linoleum. The rose-colored walls were finished with clay from another deposit. Probably Du′wa intended to occupy this room as his own private quarters. He had not yet moved his loom into it, but no doubt that would follow.

I happen to have a clue to Du'wa's age. He is four years younger than a brother who is definitely eighty-seven.

Many, many years ago, when she was a young woman, Cho'ro was already one of the skillful pottery-makers of her village, which ranks high in that craft.

The clay that she used was obtained from a deposit a half mile from her home and was carried in a square of strong fabric on her own strong back. The hard, grayish chunks were dug from a thin layer between two sandstone strata. The deposit of the best quality of clay, that which has little grit in its substance, was situated far back in the confined space. To reach it, Cho'ro had to crawl in on elbows and knees. For temper to mix in with the clay, she crushed fragments of pottery that had cracked in firing. These she ground on her metates until they were as fine as flour. The dried sheep manure that served as fuel she herself secured from the two or three corrals belonging to her family, one of them a mile or more from the village.

Once or twice a year, while her mother looked after the four small children, she set out in the early morning with an empty bag tied around her waist and visited a small deposit of coal two miles away. There she selected small, clear lumps, placed them in the bag, and carried the supply home on her back. A little coal and a few small pieces of juniper would ignite the sheep manure to start the firing of a batch of pottery.

Also once a year she descended from the mesa to the desert below and replenished her supply of tansy mustard to boil down and use with black pigment. Down there she obtained narrow yucca leaves from which she made the brushes used in painting the designs on her ware.

Shaping and firing the pottery demanded less physical labor, but the firing was exacting. Once a batch was started and the bottom layer of kindling and sheep manure was set afire, there could be no delaying. The sun-dried and decorated bowls and jars must be placed promptly and skillfully in position, along with the protecting fragments and more sheep manure. Cho'ro had to step lively, and not mind the smoke that rolled up, enveloping her face and filling her eyes.

Last of all came the trip to the trader down below the mesa, with a carefully packed burden on her back. Downhill it was, but nevertheless a task for a strong back and strong legs. Not many jars and pots are required to make a weight of forty pounds.

All of this began a very long time ago for Cho'ro, for she is today one of the oldest Hopi women. Much of the activity continued for many a year, while she was a mother, a grandmother, and a great-grandmother. The hardest parts, the securing of coal and sheep manure, and the task of carrying the finished pottery to the trader, were taken over by younger members of her family as she grew older, but the actual shaping of the pottery, its polishing and decorating, and the exacting task of firing, Cho'ro continued to do herself.

Then one day, a few years ago, Cho'ro had a fall. Although the injury seemed not to be serious, it was obscure and it failed to heal naturally or yield to treatment. Something must have happened to her spine or to some other vital part, for Cho'ro could no longer walk. With suitable support she could stand, but from the hips down she was nearly helpless.

Cho'ro's daughters and granddaughters had long since learned the art of pottery-making. They knew how to turn out

Whatever You Can Do

a product which at least approached Cho'ro's—thin-walled ware that would ring when you tapped it, that was decorated with the designs that Cho'ro had helped to perfect, and that was fired with such care and skill that burned spots seldom appeared. Their steady hands and young eyes could shape a bowl into perfect symmetry and proportions and could paint clean and accurate lines with the yucca brushes.

For Cho'ro one task remained which she could do, even while sitting on a mat on the floor or while propped up on a couch. Every piece of pottery must be polished before it is decorated and fired. The thoroughness with which this is done determines the glossy, satiny finish of the completed bowl or jar. The tool for polishing is simple: a small piece of suitable stone, perhaps half the size of an egg. The texture of this stone is extremely important. It must be capable of polishing the surface of the ware, yet must itself be glossy smooth, seemingly as smooth as glass. Cho'ro possessed two or three of these fine polishing stones which had been handed down in her family. Where they had come from originally no one knew, though certainly they were different from any stone found naturally near the village. Apparently they were pieces of lava from some distant place, perhaps from the eminence far to the north that the Hopis call Axe Mountain and that in early times was the source of stone tools.

Since several of the members of Cho'ro's family were makers of pottery, there were always many pieces to be polished. These Cho'ro took in hand. Propped up on a couch, she worked them over, giving each one full attention until every inch of surface was as smooth as the polishing stone itself. In this activity she found continuing satisfaction and the pride of accomplishment. When the pieces had been decorated and fired, she could look upon them as articles that she had helped to create.

CUYA

Her name is pronounced Kuh′-yah, and it means "To dip water." She is the wife of Maho. Born in Walpi, on First Mesa, she lives there in an ancestral home, not far from the narrow ledge that leads across to the village.

Whatever You Can Do

Today Cho'ro is more than ninety years old, perhaps almost a hundred. Certainly, she is older than some of the others whose ages can be approximated and who have seen ninety summers or more. Several years have elapsed since the time when she became unable to walk, but mentally she is alert, and her manner gives no indication of baffled or unhappy old age. She is old, but she is still productive and a contributor to the world she lives in.

Blindness came to Mak'ta without much warning. Its approach was stealthy and swift, and its results were final. If this had happened today, it might have been checked, with no permanent harm done, but at that time the remedy and the expert attention were not available.

Through more than seventy years Mak'ta's eyes had served him well. He could distinguish with certainty a far-off stray sheep, differentiating its dull gray from that of the surrounding desert where it slowly fed. A glance at a manta woven by a neighbor was enough to tell him whether the intricate pattern made by the fine yarn was accurately done. When a Navajo family came into view a mile away on the wagon road that crossed a branch of the mesa, Mak'ta could tell you who they were and how many women and children there were in the wagon. Returning late at night from herding sheep, with only the stars for light, he could always avoid the inconspicuous cactus that looked so much like the desert floor.

In the year when the trouble came upon him, his crops were well established and in good order by midsummer. The corn was more than kneehigh, and it showed, by its vigor, the reserve moisture deep in the ground and the good results of faithful cultivation. The melon plants had sent out runners two or three yards long. There was ample opportunity to take a few days off

45

for the Home Dance that was celebrated in his village toward the end of July and in a neighboring village the following week.

A few mornings later when he awoke, his eyes felt as though they were filled with hot sand. Opening and closing his eyelids was like scraping them over jagged bits of stone. Almost every spring, one or more violent sand storms had deposited painful grit in his eyes, because he could not keep them closed while working in his fields or herding his sheep. But those experiences were not like this.

Getting a cup of water, he dissolved in it a piece of the dark crystalline salt that comes from a dry lake beyond the Zuñi pueblo. With this he bathed his eyes, allowing the solution to seep under the lids as much as possible. He did not expect it to be soothing, and he was not surprised at the pain it caused. Several times that day and the next he repeated the treatment. After a few more days he repeated it again, then he gave it up, since his eyes were no better, but were growing definitely worse. The lids were swollen, and the feeling of hot sand was continuous.

At first Mak'ta was able to continue his normal activities, although it was difficult to keep his eyes open and although everything near and far seemed blurred. But when harvest time came, a month or two after the Snake Ceremony, the world was almost blotted out. He could find his way reasonably well to his fields, but could not be certain about the boundaries where a neighbor's land adjoined. A younger brother was obliged to take over and complete the harvest. At his home he could easily carry in pieces of firewood from the chip-littered spot next to the pile of juniper, but he could not attempt to do the chopping. A few days of sitting idly on the stone ledge in front of his home or visiting neighbors brought no satisfaction. Mak'ta sent again for his brother.

Together they took down the beams and accessories of

Whatever You Can Do

Mak'ta's loom from their place of storage. He had started weaving a manta the previous spring, a deep blue and black rectangular garment that is traditional among older Hopi women and is easily traded with pueblos in New Mexico. Eighteen or twenty inches had been completed, and this, together with the many strands of warp, was wrapped around the lower beam. The upper beam, to which the opposite ends of the warp were attached, was tied carefully to the lower. In the floor of Mak'ta's living room, close to a wall, two iron rings were embedded. Overhead, a stout, rigid pole was attached to the ceiling rafters. Between these two Mak'ta and his brother now affixed the loom, with the upper beam laced snugly so that the strands of warp were taut. The strip of manta already woven was smooth and rich in its deep color, its diamond, diagonal pattern unobtrusive but pleasing. The upper edge of the strip was opposite Mak'ta's shoulders as he seated himself on a mat close to the loom.

From its storage place, the brother brought a bag containing a dozen or more balls of yarn, part of them black, the rest blue. Both lots had the same history up to a point. Both represented wool from Mak'ta's own sheep, wool which he had clipped, scoured, carded, and spun. But the blue yarn was white wool that had been dyed with indigo obtained from the trader. The black yarn started as the natural color of the wool from black sheep, but it was deepened by dyeing it in a decoction that Mak'ta made from the seeds of black sunflowers, combined with ochre and gum from piñon pine, with a final smoking in a tight box in which a little yarn was smouldering.

Mak'ta picked up the balls of yarn one after another and held them to his nostrils. *"Sakwa',"* he said of the first, "blue," and *"Kwuma',"* of another, "black." The difference was faint, but it was unmistakable and the identification was reliable.

47

The Hopis

His fingers sought the top row of weft in the unfinished manta before him and traced the sequence as the yarn followed its course in and out of the warp, a certain number of strands at first, then another number, again a different number. In this way he went clear across the breadth of the fabric. Now he knew exactly where he had interrupted his weaving. Winding a new lot of yarn on the slender stick that served as a shuttle, he set to work. It was slow at first, because he had to rely solely on touch. But the knack of it came to him; the work moved along; and facility steadily increased. Day by day, slowly and surely, the fabric began to lengthen. Occasionally a neighbor came in, talked a while about village news and the prospects of rain, and observed the weaving but said nothing about it. After all Mak'ta was not the first Hopi to weave after losing his sight.

When the manta was finished, just after it had been folded and set aside, two neighbors—old men like Mak'ta—came to visit. One of them was expecting to leave soon on a trading trip to the New Mexico pueblos, although he had not spoken of this in advance. After talking of various matters, they asked if they might see the manta. As they unfolded it and spread it out, they offered no comment, but, from something in the quality of their silence, from the length of time they took in replacing the garment, Mak'ta felt their approval. He had not expected them to offer comment, favorable or otherwise. This is not the accustomed way. Whatever you have done must stand for itself, must be its own judge and jury. To condemn a thing is to create enmity and perhaps to do unjustified harm to another. To praise is to make comparisons which might cause someone else to be unhappy. As the two visitors left his door, Mak'ta's sharpened ears caught a word, "Lo'loma!" which means "Good."

A day or two later, one of the men came back to examine the

48

manta once more, and he inquired about the price. Mak'ta named a sum which a good manta ought to bring. He was not surprised when his visitor accepted.

Many times in the course of his long life, Mak'ta had woven the traditional shawl which the young Hopi woman wears on occasion, and which always finds a ready market in New Mexico pueblos, as well as nearer home. He set to work now to do one.

The task was different from that of completing the partly-woven manta. To begin with, he needed cotton yarn for the body of the shawl. This he would have to spin. But it was not difficult, for only the simple spindle was required, and he had spun so many miles of yarn in his life that he could have managed about as well with his eyes closed as with them open. He also needed a supply of red woolen yarn, and here his brother helped by attending to the dyeing, drawing on a supply of the plant which the Hopis call *hohoi'si,* which Mak'ta had collected before he became blind. Blue yarn, dyed with indigo, was already on hand.

Setting up the loom was not especially difficult. The tricky part came in changing the type of weave when the broad, blue border was completed and the adjacent red band was started, for the groundwork of the blue band was done with a diamond weave, and of the red band with a diagonal weave. In both cases the colored woolen yarn was manipulated into the fabric in the weaving itself, taking the place of cotton weft in such way that the colored band appeared solid as you looked at one side of the shawl. The central white part was cotton only, done in a diagonal weave.

Mak'ta had no trouble in distinguishing the cotton yarn from the wool. The feel was different, and the cotton had little or no odor. The blue woolen yarn was already familiar. As it

49

turned out, the red yarn had its own distinct smell from the dye.

In two or three weeks the shawl was completed, and in another week or so, it was sold.

So Mak'ta, with two articles to his credit, settled down to his blind weaving. He could do his own carding and spinning. He needed help in the dyeing, which his brother would furnish, but he required no assistance at the loom, and he could well take care of any bargaining over his finished products. He was busy, and he felt pride in his accomplishments. When he wished, he could visit other homes in the village, and he found that old friends had a way of dropping in to visit him, seemingly just to watch him at his work. Increasingly they sought his views and judgment. With fewer distractions and more time to reflect, he could ponder and weigh the merits and demerits of problems.

The ceremonies in the plaza, also, he still could enjoy, for he knew just what the participants were doing, as the familiar chants pursued their well-known course. Friends came to greet him. No one condoned with him, for that is not the Hopi way, and besides, no one felt that there was anything to condone about. He was a valued and respected citizen.

COUNTING THE YEARS

THE FACT that many of the older Hopis possess no accurate knowledge about their ages leads to an interesting quest, if you wish to discover just how old one of them may be. It does more than that, for it leads to an understanding of some Hopi views and beliefs concerning age, which are quite different from the attitude of the white man.

Until recent years, the Hopis possessed no written records of their own relating to either personal or tribal events. Their method of recording history was by word of mouth, by the medium of verbal accounts related by older men to younger as part of the Kiva instruction and training. Naturally these accounts dealt with events which, in the Hopi world, were considered to be significant, especially in the realm of traditions. The time when an individual was born would hardly qualify for such attention. An individual or some member of his family might know that his birth took place before some important tribal event, such as a period of critical drouth, but this does not mean that his birth had been set down as occurring in a certain calendar year. The white man's calendar was non-existent among the Hopis until a few decades ago.

The white man himself began keeping some individual rec-

TU'QUI

Tu'qui was born in Walpi about ninety years ago, perhaps more than ninety. His name means "Mountain,"
and is pronounced Tü'quee. In the few months since
this picture was made he has passed on to the Hopi
Spirit world.

ords of Hopi boys and girls when the first government school was established, twenty years after the Civil War. But the records were of dubious validity. Many of the young folk who entered came without specific knowledge as to their ages. Their parents simply guessed. Thus many of the older Hopis, although they attended the school at that time, have no reliable source of information concerning their ages, even if they are interested. Many others did not attend school at all. The span of time involved includes Hopis who are now in or beyond their eighties.

In more recent times the census-takers have done a lot of guessing. They could not take the time to seek out collateral information. In any case they were likely not to be especially interested. If the person interviewed said that he was sixty years old, why question his statement? If someone in the same family gave a different figure for the same person, you could take your choice. If a husband said that his wife was seventy, presumably he ought to know. If she was asked her age, there was little likelihood that she would have anything definite to offer. Thus, the records at the Indian Service headquarters may or may not be valid.

If you inquire of a middle-aged Hopi the age of his father or his old grandfather, the figure that he gives may be a well-considered estimate, or it may be a conjecture that cannot reasonably be accepted. Talking with a man one day, who must be at least in his fifties, I asked him about his father, who surely would be no less than twenty years older. He suggested sixty as the older man's age, but revised this to eighty, when I demurred. To him it was not a vitally important matter. The old man was active and well.

There is one way by which the age of some of the older Hopis can sometimes be approximated. The starting point is a friend who is well along in years and whose age can be established through some authentic record or definite event. From this you can work up or down to his older or younger brothers. He will know pretty well about them. One of these in turn may have been a playmate of the person whose age you are trying to establish. Perhaps, as young men, they made an expedition together for salt, or a trip after eagles, the older one of the pair serving as leader. Perhaps they went through their initiation together. As the circle widens others may be brought into the sequence, and eventually verification may be possible. To the Hopis this is not especially significant or worth the effort. To the white man, who is interested in the activities, views, and beliefs of older men, there is a reward.

As white men, we continually find ourselves asking a Hopi "How old is he?" even though we are aware that specific information is not available. We speculate on the age of a man or woman who appears to be very old, and automatically we ask the question because of our habitual emphasis on age. When we have done this time and again, our Hopi friend, in attempting to answer the question, gives more attention to the subject than has been his habit and may thereafter more nearly approach our way of referring to age. Also, the advent of old age pensions has given the matter of records new importance. Hopis who never before gave thought to the number of years they have lived now find that they must establish their ages, or must find means to correct a statement believed to be in error.

Nevertheless, among the older Hopis there is a point of view which, at heart, is but little changed. Briefly stated, it is this: the less you think about your age, the better off you are.

In the Hopi view, anything toward which you direct your attention is thereby made more potent. If the matter is one which is giving you happiness and well-being it can be made stronger. If it is something desirable, which has not yet taken place, it can be made more probable. If, on the other hand, it can bring unhappiness, can entail results which are not to be desired, thinking about it will only add to its strength and may bring it about.

So it is with the infirmities that can come with old age. They grow more probable and stronger whenever you think about them. You can bring them upon yourself by letting them occupy your thoughts. You can keep them at a distance, too weak to inflict themselves upon you, by refusing to give them attention.

Consciously or unconsciously all this is reflected in the physical attitude of the old folk. A man is likely to walk with as much vigor as he has. He may lie down and rest frequently and for considerable periods, but when he gets up to go somewhere with a younger visitor or to attend to an errand, he maintains a vigorous pace. More than once I have seen an old man—a man I knew to be past eighty—set out at almost a trot for the top of the mesa, six hundred feet higher and two miles away.

The demeanor of an old man, the expression of his face, and the look in his eye, is likely to be one of alertness. Along with this, there is a poise, an attitude of being at peace with the world, an expression that is the opposite of anxiety or frustration. Perhaps the bad drouth will continue, but there is corn in the storehouse. Perhaps the new road that the government is building will bring too many troublesome tourists, but all that is beyond personal control, and besides, it may work out all right. As for conflicts and wars, they are a long way off. The Hopis do not forget that their mission is peace. And, as confidence and poise help to keep the physical body strong and responsive, the active body builds confidence and poise.

On one of my visits in the home of Hona'psi, the elderly man who continues to ride many miles on his burro in order to take his turn at herding sheep, I had with me a white companion

57

with whom I have spent many days in the Hopi country. After we had left and had climbed into my companion's car, he exclaimed, "If I never had any other reward for the years I've spent in the Indian country, I've had a lot in just watching that man's face. He may work hard, and he may be old, but I don't believe that he ever even thinks about it."

A Hopi friend summed up the matter to me one time. "It's best not to think about your age," he said. "If you do, it just makes you sad."

THE DESERT PROVIDES

THEIR FAR-OFF ANCESTRAL EXPERIENCE in living off the land has left its imprint on the Hopis of today. Necessity no longer prevails to the same extent, but many of the old resources have not been forgotten, and an attitude of self-containment persists.

In those remote times, before there were any cultivated crops of consequence or any domestic animals, a family was obliged to use what it could find or could devise, if it was to survive. In one way or another, it did just that. Suitable stones, usually plentiful in the high desert country, could be laid up to form walls of a small house, crude but serviceable. Such wild animals as the desert offered could be hunted; their flesh provided food and their skins became clothing. And wild plants of various kinds added to the food supply.

As time moved along the houses were better built; native cotton provided fibers for weaving; wool was added to cotton; and cultivated crops supplemented the wild plants.

Today, a Hopi family goes to the trader for various staples; its women may wear familiar house dresses; its men wear store clothes and store shoes; it may even own and use a pickup truck; but it still bases its economy to a considerable degree on native resources. In a modified but significant way it still partially

59

lives off the land. The effects of this on Hopi bearing and character are unmistakable.

When a man sets out to build a house, he is not concerned with the wage scales that have been established by carpenters' or plasterers' unions. Some one may help him with the building, but, if so, it will be a member of his own family or a neighbor with whom he strikes up a trade. Quite likely, he will do the entire job himself. His building materials he will get largely from the desert, with the addition of some items which he must buy. He is not interested in the price of Portland cement because he can make his own excellent mortar out of clay and sand, both of which he knows just where to find, and this mortar will serve well in laying up his well-built stone walls. He needs no package material from a store for the inside finish of his walls, because another native clay deposit can supply that.

When his house is completed, he will not be concerned with the prevailing price of anthracite coal or fuel oil. He will use juniper for cooking and will obtain it from the high mesa country to the north, farther away than formerly but, nevertheless, still available. The coal that he uses for heating will come from one of the deposits in the reservation, probably from one near by, where the coal is exposed and may be had for the digging. As for fuel oil, a pipe line crosses the desert, south of the reservation, but no branch leads to the Hopi villages, nor is one likely to do so in the predictable future. Its content is bound for cities, where houses have furnaces and where there are factories; its price per gallon is of no interest to the Hopis.

Except in very old homes, especially those occupied by very old persons, the furnishings of a house, once derived entirely from the neighboring desert, are likely now to include various manufactured articles. Even the old folk are not unresponsive to

60

the comfort and convenience which these can contribute, although the appeal may not be compelling. The list will probably include a table, a cookstove, a bed or two, three or four chairs, and, with these manufactured articles, one or two low stools that the householder himself has made. A cupboard or sometimes a kitchen cabinet may be added to the list, but seldom will there be more than two beds. If more sleeping space is needed, sheep skins can be unrolled on the floor.

Along with the manufactured articles, traditional products of the desert persist. The metates for grinding corn, though used perhaps less often now, have not been forgotten. Neither has the little bundle of long, slender stems of purple hair grass, that serves for brushing the partly-ground cornmeal into proper position on the grinding stone. When the bundle is reversed and the stiff grass stems are spread out it also serves as a strainer.

The essentials for the traditional crafts of the women are derived almost solely from the surrounding country, just as they were centuries ago. The near-by desert provides clay for the pottery that the women of First Mesa produce. Also, it provides the pigments for decorating the pottery, the yucca brushes for applying the pigments, the fuel, the wood, and the bit of coal and the dried sheep manure, for the final firing. The desert supplies the yucca for binder and the galleta grass for filler, which the women of Second Mesa require in making their handsome coiled baskets. It provides the materials they use in dyeing some of the yucca strips black and some of them Indian red, thus making possible the designs achieved in fashioning the baskets. In the villages of Third Mesa and at Moenkopi, the wickerwork baskets and plaques are woven with peeled and dyed stems of rabbit brush and the native plant which the Hopis call *si'wi,* both of them products of the desert. Throughout the Hopi country, the crafts

KU'KUAM'

Her name is pronounced Kuh'-kya-ahm', and means
"Older sister." She is one of the oldest of Hopi women,
probably just over one hundred. In spite of her age,
she is eagerly active in those household duties which
she can perform. Her home is in the village of Sichomovi, on First Mesa—the same house in which she was
born.

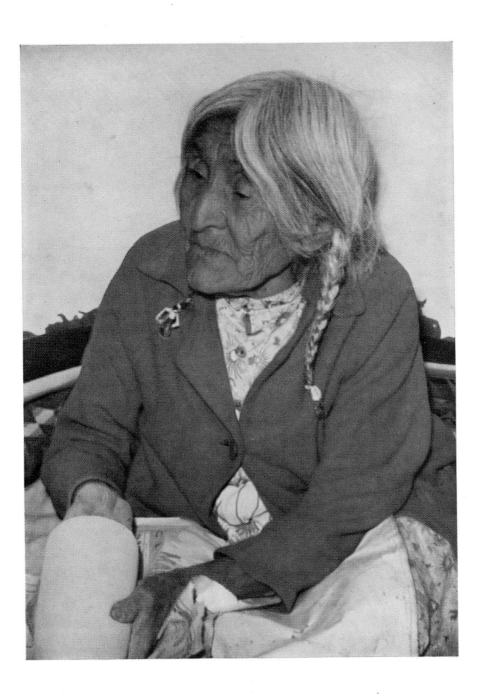

of the women are independent of commercial supplies or manufactured devices.

The story of men's craft is varied. Weaving, an ancient art, is still done on a loom devised from native materials. The weaver uses no factory-made machine. His woolen yarn comes from sheep pastured on the range, and is dyed partially with products of the desert, and partially with commercial materials. For blue he uses indigo which has long been stocked by the traders. He knits footless woolen socks in the same familiar way of our own grandmothers. Cotton, however, which he requires for certain textiles, no longer is raised in his fields as it used to be, many years ago. He buys it and then cards it and spins it.

A considerable number of Hopi men carve and decorate Kachina dolls in their spare time. Some of the dolls find their way to the traders or to other outlets, thus adding to cash income. Only the paint and some of the feathers do not originate in the desert. Moccasin leather may be a Hopi's own product, but it is likely to be purchased at the trader's or acquired in barter.

If the man is one of the relatively few Hopis who works in silver, he must depend largely on materials and accessories which his own near-by desert cannot offer. His sheet silver he buys, but his turquoise he is likely to acquire in the form of rough pieces, matrix and all, and these he grinds down on a hand grinder to develop whatever gem materials a piece may possess. A tank of compressed gas is essential for his soldering, and of course has to be purchased.

Thus, for the men of the Hopi family, some dependence upon resources beyond the desert has crept in, especially in making articles to sell, although in other ways the desert still provides.

Hunting, as a means of acquiring meat for the table, may never have been as productive for the Hopis and their ancestors as it was for Indians who lived in wooded and well-watered regions where game was abundant. However, some of the larger animals, such as deer and antelope, were available to the Hopis, as well as the universal rabbit. Today only the rabbit remains in large numbers in the country surrounding the Hopi villages. But rabbit hunts are by no means neglected or forgotten. They are joint enterprises, a sort of free-for-all in which all the men of a village who care to do so, young or old, take part. Some sort of decision is arrived at that a hunt will take place on a certain day. An announcement is made, or the word just gets around. Perhaps the prime reason for the hunt is the damage that rabbits are doing to crops, or perhaps it is simply time to have a hunt.

When the day arrives men hurry off to the designated area by any means available. Many go on foot, although horseback is preferable. In fact, a visitor would likely be surprised at the number of horses that seem to materialize out of the empty desert. Some of the men have guns, others are armed only with clubs or throwing sticks. A trader, even at a distance, becomes aware of an impending hunt because of a sudden demand for ammunition. Having arrived at the chosen spot, the whole outfit spreads out and starts a drive, converging, perhaps, toward a center or toward a natural barrier. Presently, the men with throwing sticks and clubs have a chance. So the hunt goes on until an area has been covered and the rabbits have been killed or have escaped. Everybody has had a good time, tender growing vegetables are saved from further damage, and dangling rabbits are carried back home. Miraculously, in spite of the excitement, nobody gets shot.

A Hopi family pays more attention than we do to wild plants that can supplement diet. They do not depend on these resources, but they do not neglect them. There is no fruit and vegetable market around the corner from a Hopi home.

The Desert Provides

An elderly Hopi friend and I wandered around over the mesa one day looking up and discussing wild plants. Later we did the same thing in the sandy country down below. When there was opportunity, I asked a grandmother friend about the present-day use of these various plants and about her opinion as to their palatability in these times of cultivated products.

As my elderly companion and I went about our exploratory walks, we promptly found a number of subjects for discussion. A shoulder-high, grayish shrub with compact and spiny-stiff branches attracted my attention. "That's *su'ovi*," said my friend. "We burn small branches of it and mix the ashes with blue corn-meal when we make blue piki. It makes the color stay nice and blue, and it makes the taste better." I knew that something like this is the standard practice. The alkaline character of the ashes prevents the blue from fading or changing to a pinkish hue. The shrub, the four-wing saltbush, was abundant.

Another shrub near by, equally tall but with straight, slender, deep green stems that grew in clusters as if tied together at the base, looked more like a source of interesting desert food but could not qualify. This was Mormon tea. "Did the Mormons use it for tea?" I asked. "Maybe," said my friend. "I don't think so." Later, he pointed out a plant which in fact has been used, at times, in Hopi homes to make a sort of tea. Its Hopi name is *hohoi'si*. The flowers are commonly used to make a yellow dye. This color is changed over to a brownish red by smoking the dyed article. The young, tender leaves of the plant are the part used for tea. "I've tasted it," said my friend. "It's pretty good."

My grandmother-friend had some further observations to offer on native tea. There is another plant, she said, which is something like *hohoi'si,* but better. The leaves grow flat on the ground, and the little flowers are orange. It is not conspicuous,

67

and you might think that it is scarce, but if you know what to look for you can easily find it, and the tender leaves make a nice hot drink. She called it by its Hopi name, *si'ta.*

A shrub, a sumac, often called the squawbush, offers abundant reward. Its red berries are used in making a "lemonade," and are widely sought for that purpose. "We use it a lot," declared the companion of my walks. He called the berries *suvi'fsi.* Another red berry, which he called *keve'fsi,* helped out long ago, during a period of crop failures. The taste is inclined to be bitter. The berry was made more palatable by first boiling it and mashing it into a paste. After that a clay which is mildly alkaline was worked up with water to make a sort of cream, and this was used with the berries. The combination may still be used occasionally, but is not in favor. Still another berry, a wild currant, may be tried by some one who is rash, but is definitely not approved. "It will give you a bellyache," warned my friend.

It was in the realm of greens and potherbs that we found our most varied specimens. Apparently, the Hopis have tried almost everything, in the course of the centuries, and have made many discoveries.

The plant that is available earliest in the spring, the tansy mustard, which they call by the simple name *a'sa,* is widely used. Another, a relative which grows among the rocks on the cliffs and is considered superior, is much less plentiful and, possibly for that reason, is especially sought. Perhaps the most abundant plant used in this way is the Rocky Mountain beeweed, *tu'mi* the Hopis call it, conspicuous through the summer because of its purple flowers, favored by humming birds. When the plant is quite young and tender it is boiled, as we would prepare spinach. Around the cultivated fields, this plant, which otherwise would be suppressed as a weed, is likely to be given sanctuary. It is one of the most favored of wild plants and is considered to have a superior flavor. Bunches of it are hung up to dry for winter use and are often to be seen in a Hopi home.

The various shrubs which we call saltbush are scattered over the desert. These are different from the four-wing saltbush which contributes ashes for blue piki. The saltbushes provide tender leaves in the early spring, and these are sometimes gathered and used in cookery. "They taste a little salty," said my companion. "Not too much but just a little. They give a nice flavor." As with the beeweed, the tender shoots, with their appetizing leaves, are tied in bundles, bound with yucca, and hung on an outside wall to be dried by the sun.

In a sandy hollow below the mesa, we ran across a shrub which has a different and valued appeal. The slender shoots were vivid green and carried tiny, blue flowers. My companion was enthusiastic about its flavor. He broke off a shoot and nibbled its tender tip. "This one is always good," he said. "Everybody likes it. It's the first thing green in the spring. You can cook it or you can eat it without cooking. It isn't scarce, either. You can find it most anywhere. You can dry it, too, if you want to, and have it all winter." The aroma of the small leaves, when crushed, was unmistakable. This shrub is a member of the mint family.

Another representative of the same family, found in many places, is the plant which we call bee balm and which the Hopis call *nana'kofsi*. A little dried bundle, hanging beside the door of a home which I visited, told the story of its part in winter cookery.

I asked my grandmother-friend if she and her neighbors still made use of the plant which the Hopis call *wi'wa,* a member of the amaranth family. "Oh yes," she said, "quite a lot. If you gather it before it gets too big, you can cook it the same as you would spinach. It's good, too, if you cook it with meat."

Some of the wild plants and their uses that my companion and I were discussing were reminiscent of practices related to us by our own grandmothers, who happened to live in rural areas. They, too, sought the tang of early dandelion greens, the piquant flavor of young mustard plants, or the tasty marsh marigolds. But other plants that my Hopi friend and I examined were only in the province of the desert and its people. The plants themselves had no familiar English name.

This was true regarding a small plant with yellow flowers which the Hopis call *tui'tsma*. "We don't cook that one," explained my friend. "Sometimes we mash it up in water and then sprinkle that on popped corn. Sometimes we use it with roasted corn. Sometimes we just eat it as it is. We can dry it, too, and save it for winter."

I had once photographed a striking little plant that grew no more than a few inches high and that bore a handsome pink blossom, almost as wide across as the height of the plant. This turned out to be another example of the desert's store of flavors. It is used with dishes made with corn or sometimes with meat, as we use the herbs that we buy in a store or raise in our gardens.

Rarely a Hopi cook flavors a dish with one or another of the wild onions that can be collected here and there. No doubt, this practice is ancient, and probably the wild plant was used more freely in former times than now, because cultivated onions can now be raised in a Hopi garden.

When I first learned that many years ago, in times of food scarcity, the Hopis collected the seeds of wild plants and used them as a source of meal, just as corn is normally used, I wondered at the labor that, seemingly, this must have involved. Gathering wild seeds in appreciable quantities appeared to be a superhuman task, but the Hopi country has three or four species of plants which grow freely and which can be used for food, if there be need. Two of these my friend and I found in abundance as we wandered around in the sandy country below the mesa. They are grasses, and they carry aloft large, open panicles. One of them grows to two or three feet tall, and the other twice that height. Both are called dropseeds, and both have an obliging way about them. When the seeds are ripe, they will fall in a shower, if the stem of the panicle is struck or shaken. All that is necessary to catch the seeds is something beneath the panicle, a cloth or a tight basket. Although the seeds themselves are small, a panicle will hold a very large number. A third species, called the alkali sacaton, is similarly utilized.

"We can use them," said my friend, "if we need to. We can grind the seeds and mix the meal with cornmeal to sweeten up the wild flavor. We don't do it now, but we could. There are plenty of plants, and we all know how to use them."

"How about the prickly-pear cactus?" I asked. "Yes," he said, "we still use the joints sometimes, if they are young. But they must be young and tender. First you have to get rid of the spines. You can burn most of them off. Then you boil the joint. Then you dip it in some kind of sweet syrup."

Here, again, my grandmother-friend had an observation to offer. "A Navajo woman," she said, "was camped near my home. She had collected some young joints of prickly pear. First thing in the morning she started a fire and put the cactus joints on to boil. She kept on boiling them all day. Then she took them out of the water and picked off the spines. They were easy to remove. Then she cut up the joints in small pieces, sprinkled a

SI'TAIMA

A patriarch among the Hopis of First Mesa, his age is
given by his son as either ninety-seven or -eight. His
name is pronounced See'-teye-mah, and means "Flower
looked over." For many years he was Sun Watcher for
the Winter Solstice ceremony and then became head
of the ceremony. In spite of his years, he is still busily
active in the duties that lie within his strength.

little sugar on them, and they were ready to eat. They looked pretty good, prepared that way, so in a day or two we tried it. We found that they were really good, very good."

Thinking about some related spiny plants that grow in Hopi country, I asked my companion who shared my walks about the hedgehog cactus.

"We use that sometimes," he said. "Just the fruit, not the plant. When I was a little fellow, we used it a lot for sweetening, along with cornmeal. At that time there were no white people around. No salt in a store, nor sugar, nor flour. Now we don't have to use these fruits for sweetening, but if we need to we can. We know how."

"How about the cholla cactus fruits?"

"They used those one time. They boiled them and used them with other foods. Once in a while somebody does that now. But it's mostly for time of famine."

My companion's reply to my next remark was emphatic. "I've been told," I said, "that Hopi children will chew a cattail head along with tallow, as a sort of chewing gum." My friend shook his head. "That's not Hopi," he declared. "That's Piaute. They chew the stalks too." Clearly this practice was nothing to claim with pride.

"There's something else," I continued. "Another substitute that I've heard of for chewing gum. How about the little 'berries' on cottonwood trees?"

"Well, the kids chew them sometimes. But not much. That's mostly Paiute too."

As a matter of fact, where cottonwood trees are within reach, Hopi youngsters *are* likely to pick off the "berries" and chew them. The practice is not wholly alien.

We spoke, then, of the fruits of the broad-leaved yucca, which

75

is found in many parts of the desert. The Navajos sometimes gather these and bake them in an earth pit. But the Hopis, it appears, seldom use them, perhaps in part for the reason that this species of yucca is more plentiful in regions outside the Hopi country.

Another wild food, however, is unquestionably in use and in favor among the peoples of the northern desert, including the Hopis. This is the seed, or the so-called "nut," of the piñon pine. This compact tree grows abundantly in the higher altitudes, including some parts of Black Mesa, on the southern borders of which the Hopi villages are situated, as well as neighboring mountain slopes. The little brown seeds are broadcast by the cones when ripe. When there is opportunity, the Hopis gather the seeds; if not, they are likely to acquire a supply by trading.

One evening, visiting in a Hopi home, I watched the householder gently roasting some of the "nuts." He had placed them in a broad, shallow pan. Sitting before the open oven door, he adjusted the position of the pan so that the nuts would brown slowly while he stirred them with a stick. They did not require roasting to be edible; the process simply gave them a slightly different flavor.

On another day, I was visiting with a friend in one of the villages high up on Second Mesa. As we left the house to ride down in a small truck, my friend handed me a dish of a grayish, crystalline material to carry down to a relative in the lower village. The dish was surprisingly heavy. The grayish substance in it was salt from the dry lake beyond the Zuñi reservation. Even though store salt is available at the trader's, and even though it is used and is cheap, the native material is still sought and preferred for some uses in cookery.

"It has more flavor," my friend explained. "You don't need

to use much of it. Just a little in a mutton stew will make the stew taste good. We had a supply one time and we used it in all our cooking. It made everything taste good."

A Hopi friend, who had just returned from the salt lake, had a new experience to relate when I ran across him recently on First Mesa.

"It's too bad," he said. "The Hopi people have always gone to the lake for salt. They must have been doing it for hundreds of years, long before there were any whites in this country. Now a white man claims that he owns the lake. He is charging for the salt, so much a pound. If you don't pay him you can't have any."

So the Hopi family continues to turn to the desert, in spite of what the white man offers or takes away, in spite of packaged foods, store bread, and cartons of salt. They have not forgotten. In the midst of a land that offers no rich verdure, no running streams or lush meadows, they nevertheless can find, if they choose or if need be, the essentials for a house to live in, fuel for warmth, work to do with hands, and a considerable part of the food to sustain life.

HOPI DOCTOR

IT WAS THE WINTER of the big snows. Far to the north, in the vast ranges of Wyoming and Montana, cattle stood helpless against the icy blasts and died where they stood. Over the table-land of northern Arizona, airplanes winged, dropping bales of hay for hapless sheep and bags of flour and cases of condensed milk for stranded Navajo families.

As I crossed the high mesa, on my way to the Hopi agency, sixty miles north of the railway, I passed through a snow-buried country, where gaunt junipers raised twisted arms out of an enveloping whiteness. As our truck descended the long and winding hill, where the narrow road is cut sharply out of precipitous slopes, we were glad to be shod with chains that held us to our course.

At the agency, the superintendent sat before an improvised switchboard, directing emergency operations. Phoenix wanted to know whether trucks could get through the reservation and by what road. The man who was directing the airplane movements asked instructions as to the next day's flights. How was a pilot who was unacquainted with the country to know when he was over that spot which they called Hard Rock? Could he follow a highway there? No? Well, what did it look like?

Hopi Doctor

The news came in that the road over Howell Mesa was completely blocked. This was the one route out of the reservation toward the west. There was danger that someone might have been caught there or would soon be. Many miles of nothingness separate Howell Mesa from the last reservation village, in one direction, and the next settlement, in the other. Could a snow plow be sent? It could, but it would be of no use. The situation on the Mesa called for heavy equipment—something like a bulldozer. I did not then know that events involving a Hopi friend were indeed taking place on that blizzard-ridden height. When I went to bed at eleven o'clock, the superintendent was still at work before his switchboard.

There was busy activity the next day in the Agency garage and in the open-air yard for road machinery. For that matter, urgent activity had been going on every day for several weeks, and many items of equipment were already at work in various places, but the big question now was the Howell Mesa problem, too far away for normal procedures and too large in proportion for the usual apparatus.

A huge bulldozer stood in the snowy yard, its big steel blade outthrust in front of its massive body. It could tackle any snowdrift, if it were on the spot where needed. But fifty miles of desert road lay between it and the buried height. To travel that distance on its own slow tractor treads would take an impossibly long time. The giant had to be transported to its task by swifter means.

An auxiliary motor cranked up the cold engine of the bulldozer. When it was warmed up, a garage man backed it out and drove it clanking to a place where a road, held in place by a stone wall, bordered a lower area which could be reached from a branch road. Another garage man drove a heavy-duty trailer into this area and backed it up against the wall. Cautiously the bulldozer

79

was run onto the trailer with no more than a few inches to spare. All these moves consumed two hours or more.

Then the garage men brought into service a great, heavy truck with multiple drive wheels, shod with chains. They backed this up to the trailer, hitched on, turned loose the roaring power of the engine, and started up. The iron-shod wheels spun on the ice and snow, but the trailer with its heavy load refused to move.

After an hour of fruitless attempts another expedient was tried. A caterpillar tractor came clanking down to the sunken area and hitched onto the front of the truck. The two pulled jointly. The trailer moved a few inches. The struggle continued. At noon the trailer had been moved a few feet, but available space in which the tractor-truck-trailer combination could maneuver was exhausted. In midafternoon they were still working at the threefold problem of ice, restricted space, and a baffling hookup. I left soon afterwards for my quarters in another part of the reservation and did not learn how the problem was solved.

That evening, by the light of the half-moon that was riding high in the frosty sky, I stumbled across frozen ruts to the home of my friend To'chi. I found him preparing for bed, although the hour was early. He looked worn out.

"I just got back," he said. "We were up on Howell Mesa. Maybe tomorrow I'll tell you about it."

The next day I called again and heard the story.

It began ten days before. A blizzard was threatening, the wind was blowing, and snow was riding on the wind. In the afternoon a Navajo drove up to To'chi's door, in a pickup truck. He had come to get To'chi to go with him to his hogan which was 150 miles away, near the precipitous base of Navajo Mountain. His wife was ill and he wanted help.

Now To'chi is a Hopi doctor. If I were to speak of him as a

medicine man you would be likely to have a wrong conception. When I used those words one time in talking with a neighbor who was visiting in my home, she said, "Does he use magic in treating his patients?"

"If you mean," I said, "does he give heed to the patient's thoughts, as well as his body? the answer is yes. But if you are thinking of witchcraft and mumbo jumbo, the answer is no."

To'chi asked the Navajo many questions. As a considerable number of Hopis do he speaks the Navajo language well enough to carry on a ready conversation. How old was the man's wife? How long had she been ill? Was she suffering any pain? Where? Was the pain just the same all the time, or did it come and go? Did she feel hot? How many children did she have? How old was the last one? Why did they come for To'chi? Did they believe that he could help the woman? Did she believe that he could help her?

After a while, To'chi went into another room where he keeps his stock of medicines, each of them derived from some one of various desert plants. Thoughtfully, he selected a dozen or more: the dried leaves of this one and that one, the roots of another, the pulverized beans of another—this last to be used only in emergency, for it was potent and too much of it would be dangerous. He must have with him a good many different medicines, because he could not be sure what the trouble was until he could see the patient and study her condition. It was essential to take along a stock of each because he could not come back for more. It was necessary to carry a larger supply of some medicines than of others, because some had to be used in larger quantity.

With a folded blanket and his box of medicines, he joined the Navajo at the truck. The afternoon was well along, and darkness would come in an hour. The wind still blew strongly, but the

DUWA'KUKU

His age is eighty-nine or ninety. His name means
"Sand foot" and is pronounced Dü-wah'-kuh-kuh. He
was born in the village of Sichomovi, but he lives in
that part of the First Mesa which is called Tewa, or
Hano. Regardless of age, he is still active in his farming operations, travelling many miles to his fields.

snow had stopped. They set out and drove on into the night. Some time after midnight they reached the Navajo's hogan. To'chi went to bed on a sheepskin on the earth floor.

In the morning, while the Navajo boiled coffee and prepared fried cakes, To'chi quietly watched the sick woman. Stretched out on an improvised bed, she was restless, turning from one side to the other. Her dark skin was flushed. Clearly, she was running a fever.

After he had finished his breakfast, To'chi sat down beside her and talked with her about her children. "That youngest boy of yours," he said, "is getting to be a big fellow. He'll be helping his father herd sheep pretty soon. Next time you go to town he'll be wanting you to bring him a pair of those cowboy boots."

A loom leaning against the wall held a rug that was nearly finished. To'chi stepped over to it and looked it over, while the woman's eyes followed him. "That's a handsome pattern," he said. "Not much more to do on it. Next week you can finish it and take it to the trader's. He'll give you good money for a rug like that, enough to buy some dress goods and the cowboy boots for your son."

In To'chi's box of medicines there was one that was always good for fever. He could take care of that condition. Then he could set to work on the next measure that his patient needed. He emptied the grounds from the coffeepot, rinsed it, poured a cupful of water into it, and placed it on the stove. From his box he took a paper bag containing a supply of dried leaves, brownish in color and faintly aromatic. He placed a handful of these in an empty pan. When the water was boiling he poured it over the leaves, stirring them with a twig. After waiting for ten or fifteen minutes, he drained the infusion into a clean cup. He held this to the woman's lips and had her drink half of the contents.

The Hopis

"You'll feel better after you drink this," he assured her and smiled when she shuddered at the bitter taste. As he knew by experience, the bitterness was no disadvantage. If it had no more taste than water, it would seem to have no power to effect a cure. Two hours later, he gave her the remaining contents of the cup and was encouraged to note that she seemed to be somewhat less restless and to have less fever.

But the case was not to be so easily won. By nightfall, the patient was definitely worse, and when morning came, she was a very sick woman indeed. To'chi began to work then in resolute earnest. Out of his long experience, he planned the course to follow. He must take one step at a time. If the remedy that seemed to be indicated failed to bring satisfactory improvement in a reasonable length of time, the reason must be that it was not quite the right one or not potent enough. He would change then to another that was adapted to meet the conditions, though operating in a different way. In due time he would succeed. Meanwhile, he would steadily maintain the patient's confidence, because that was essential if the medicine was to have an opportunity to bring about a cure.

For three days To'chi maintained his vigil, usually sitting near the sick woman. Twice he changed to a different medicine, and twice he increased the strength of the one that he was administering. On the morning of the fourth day, he felt that a change in her condition had begun. It was not a big improvement as yet, but it was the first step. On the following morning, there was no question as to the change for the better. The patient was no longer uneasy, no longer showing signs of fever. In fact, the restlessness of sickness had given way to that of a person who would soon be eager to be up and about. By nightfall, he knew

86

that his work was finished. He told the Navajo that he would be ready to start for home the following morning.

In the night another blizzard came, the fourth of the record-breaking winter. Although it began slowly, it promised to increase, and in due time made good its promise. Their start for To'chi's village was delayed, because the Navajo had to attend to his sheep and then do some necessary work on his truck. The morning was half over when they drove away. In a last minute visit, To'chi noted with satisfaction that his patient was now sitting before her loom.

The first part of their journey, crossing the plateau that stretches south from Navajo Mountain, gave them no trouble. The wind can bring snow there, but it can also blow it away. The next stretch, where the narrow road crosses rocky gullies and skirts the edge of a deep canyon, was not so easy but was accomplished without undue delay. Beyond that, the long pull across the open desert, although it had to be made in the face of the wind, involved no drifts that could not readily be passed. By noon they were half way to their destination. They stopped at a trading post to buy a can of tomatoes and a box of crackers. With good luck they would reach To'chi's home by dark.

Then came a stretch of another dozen miles where the graded road did not encourage drifts. Although they were traveling now with the wind instead of against it, they could see that its violence was increasing and that the snow was getting heavier. Beyond this, the road was not graded and straight, but twisted about in the midst of little hills and hollows. Several times, where a hollow was filled with a drift, they were compelled to avoid it, detouring over sage and rabbit brush. Their progress was definitely slowed down.

The Hopis

Gradually, the road gained in altitude as it climbed to the high tableland of Howell Mesa. Presently, scattered small junipers appeared and then larger ones, growing more closely together. These broke the force of the wind, but the eddies in their lee caught the snow and piled it up. The road, although buried, could be followed with the eye, even though one were not familiar with its course; they were in no danger of becoming lost. But the truck was now in trouble. Suddenly it stalled as it plunged its nose into a drift. The Navajo driver backed it out and tried again, without success. Sizing up a possible alternate course through the junipers, he plunged in on that and again made the road, a hundred yards farther along. Here again an impossible drift soon blocked the way. Once more a detour, and once more an opening where the road must be. Two more of these maneuvers, and they had gained perhaps half a mile.

Climbing out of the truck they found the snow halfway between knee and thigh and they realized that it was steadily increasing. There was no possibility that they could drive through to the Hopi villages, nor could they backtrack. With night coming on, the temperature dropping, and the snow two or three feet deep, they could not attempt to cover the many miles to the nearest village on foot. "If we had some matches we could build a fire," To'chi remarked. The Navajo only shook his head.

The cab of the truck, none too weather-tight, offered a degree of protection from the wind and a place to sit. They unfolded To'chi's blanket, sat close together, and wrapped it around them as best they could, but it was not big enough for two persons.

"Maybe they'll come tomorrow with a snow-plow," To'chi suggested. But he knew that something more than a plow would be required to break through the deep drifts that surrounded them. Farther along, yes, where the road follows open country at lower altitude, but not high up, where the junipers grow. Through the long night, they waited in the cab, getting what warmth they could from the single blanket. There was nothing else to do.

"How about your feet?" I asked, when To'chi was telling me about the experience.

"Oh, we just kept pounding them on the floor."

Morning brought no change except that the wind had moderated a little and less snow was falling. The day wore on. Three or four times they got out of the cab and tramped back and forth next to the truck. This gave them exercise and change of position but made them feel the cold all the more when they climbed back to their seat. By nighttime the wind had stopped, the snow had ceased falling, and brilliant stars spattered the sky.

"I think maybe they'll be coming tomorrow," To'chi said, but doubted it even as he spoke.

Another sunrise brought another day with nothing to mark it as different from its predecessor. Slowly another night settled down on the stranded pair, the third since the storm had overtaken them, the third also since the can of tomatoes and the box of crackers.

With the coming of daylight, To'chi made up his mind. Climbing down from the cab, he started out on foot in the midst of the cedars, taking a winding course which permitted him to avoid the deeper drifts. In half an hour he came upon the tracks of sheep crossing the route that he was following.

"I knew that there must be a hogan somewhere," he said to me. "I figured that the sheep must have been heading in that direction. So I followed the tracks."

Probably the sheep had passed the day before, after the wind stopped. Their trail led on and on, a mile, two miles. Emerging

89

then from the cedars, it led straight to the snow-covered dome of a hogan. Smoke was rising from the short chimney. As To'chi drew near, a Navajo opened the door and stepped out. In a moment To'chi was inside, warming his hands and body at the hot sheet-iron stove. There was hot coffee in the coffeepot and a fried cake in the skillet. Without asking any questions or offering any comment, the Navajos passed these to To'chi.

After that the situation was soon explained. The two Navajos went out to their corral and saddled three horses, while the wife of one prepared more coffee. They tied coiled ropes to two of the saddles. With Navajos mounted on two of the horses, and To'chi on the third, they made ready to set out. One of the Navajos carried a long-handled shovel across the saddle in front of him, the other an axe. To'chi carried the pot of coffee and two fried cakes that the woman had wrapped up in a paper. Without difficulty, they found their way to the truck.

First they shoveled out the snow from beneath the engine of the truck and cleared a space a few feet to one side. In this space, To'chi built a fire, using dry pieces of juniper. His companion thawed out by the fire. When the bright flames had died down, he shoved the glowing coals under the truck, beneath the engine.

"I've done that lots of times," he explained to me in relating the episode. "It warms up the engine and helps it to start."

Meanwhile, the Navajos cut down a juniper that grew straight and strong. They attached one of their ropes to the lower end and the other to the top, laying the tree crosswise just in front of the truck. Each rope was led straight forward to the saddle of a horse. Climbing into the saddles, they started up, dragging the tree in its crosswise position, thus breaking a trail. Their plow did not work down as far as the ground, but it reduced the depth of snow sufficiently to provide a road that the truck could use. They continued across the mesa until they came to the region where the junipers thinned out and there were no more deep drifts. Beyond that point, the truck, with its high road clearance, could manage.

By the time they returned, To'chi's warm-up fire had made good. The truck engine, which had refused to turn over before, now responded slowly to the starter and, presently, was running in good shape. With a little more assistance from the shovel, the truck pulled out and, without too much difficulty, made its way across the mesa, down to better going. By early evening, To'chi was home, and his Navajo companion had found a place to stay for the night, before undertaking the return journey.

A Hopi doctor's call! Eight days—two days and three nights without food, caught on a high mesa in a blizzard, with a single blanket for two men! Admittedly a strenuous trip, as To'chi agreed, probably the toughest in his thirty-five years of experience. As for the length of time with the patient, that was not at all unusual. Sometimes a visit requires far more than a week.

When To'chi was a small boy his father taught him many facts about the desert. It is best, he said, that a boy know everything that he can about the things he sees. Riding along on their way to herd sheep, he would call attention to a clay bank that would make good mortar or to a ledge where good building stones could be secured. Often he would point out a plant with which the boy was unfamiliar, would have him repeat its Hopi name, and would emphasize the characteristics by which it could be recognized. If the plant could be turned to some good service, he would make that clear. But even if not, the boy must be able

NAVA′YOI YAVA

Pronounced Nah-vah′-yoi-yā-vah, his name means "Big snow falling." Usually he is known by a shortened form, Yava, often as Albert Yava. His exceptional command of both English and Hopi has led to his frequent service as an interpreter in important conferences. His education included a course in industrial art in Chicago. His age is sixty-five. His reservation home is in the village of Tewa, often spoken of as Hano, but he has a working home in the Colorado River reservation.

to identify it, for there might be a use of which the father was unaware.

Sometimes they came upon a plant which the Hopis employ as a home remedy for troubles that do not require the services of a medicine man. The common juniper was one of these. You can make a tea of the leaves, the father explained. You can use it for a laxative. Or you can mix the juniper and the sand sagebrush, *hova'kpi* he called it, and make a tea of that; also it is good for indigestion, when you have eaten too much. But if you use the sage that is called *wi'kwapi* and make a tea of that, it will make you throw up.

The shrub which we call Mormon tea was growing everywhere. Some of the old men, the father said, chew the green shoots when their gums shrink and their teeth get loose. They claim that this makes their teeth get tight again. Another plant, which he identified carefully for the boy, is used for sore lips, when the leaves are dried and powdered. Snakeweed tea also is useful for the bellyache. It feels hot and stops the pain.

When they made a long trip together to get firewood, many miles to the north in higher country, they were in the midst of scattered piñon pines. Piñon gum is useful, the father pointed out. You can melt it and make things waterproof with it, and you can use it on cuts to help them heal. Some of the bare ledges have grayish patches, a common lichen, *owa'si,* the father called it, a plant that grows on *o'wa,* a rock. The old folks, he said, used to powder this and use it on sore places on their skin.

There were other simple home remedies. When the father severely bruised the end of a finger one day, he made a little fire of dry corncobs and held his finger repeatedly in the heat and smoke as long as he could stand it. That will stop the hurt, he explained, and keep the finger from turning dark. When one of the children had a sore throat, the mother produced a little lump of the crude salt from the dry lake and had the youngster hold it in his mouth while it slowly dissolved.

More than once as father and son went about their duties the older man cautioned the boy about home remedies. "These medicines," he said, "are just for little troubles. If anything serious is wrong, the medicine man is the one to prescribe. He will know what to use. I wouldn't know."

When To'chi was twenty-five years old, a friend who was a medicine man, trained in desert remedies, visited their home. He talked first to To'chi's father. "You have taught your son," he said, "to recognize many desert plants. Some of these are for serious sickness, although you would not know about that. Many more which you do not recognize or call by name are useful. To know about all of these and to know what they are good for and how to use them requires long and hard study and instruction, such as I had when I was young. Not many young men are capable of that training. I have been observing your son, and I think that he can do it. I would like to train him."

They sent for To'chi and told him of the conversation. "If you want to do it," said the visitor, "we'll go ahead. You must understand that it will be hard work."

It was agreed, and soon the training began. Together, the two men made many trips to various parts of the desert and, sometimes, to regions far beyond the reservation, where an essential plant grew which could not be obtained at any nearer point. There were certain plants that had to be collected in the spring of the year, others in the fall; certain ones were suitable only after prolonged drouth, others only after rain. With some, the leaves are the useful part, with others, the seeds or the roots.

Hopi Doctor

To'chi learned that a familiar shrub, such as the cliff rose, may have a function that he had never suspected. He found that he must be able to distinguish among several plants which look much alike but actually are different and have different properties. He learned that many desert plants contain substances which, in sufficient quantity, are poisonous and dangerous, and therefore must be administered with caution. They are important in treating certain ailments, but you must know how to use them. The common lupine and the familiar larkspur are examples. Other plants which he had seen all his life, when collected at the right time and administered correctly, were stimulants that could almost call back from the border of death one who was very ill.

"To'chi," I said to him one time, "you must use a good many kinds of plants."

"Yes," he said, "more than a hundred kinds."

Instruction in the recognition of symptoms proceeded with the work on remedies. He must be able to study a patient, to observe his reactions, and to draw sound conclusions as to the cause of his illness. Several times To'chi's teacher took him along when visiting a patient, but for the most part, the instruction involved detailed descriptions which To'chi had to repeat and memorize.

There was no textbook or reference book to assist him in studying or to refer to at some later time when he was faced with a difficult case. The details of symptoms had to be remembered so fully and so clearly that a trustworthy picture would be always at his command to guide him in determining the cause of the illness and the remedy that would apply. He must be ready for the further knowledge which only experience can provide and, meanwhile, must skillfully serve the patients who trust themselves to his care.

The Hopis

All this required months of concentrated work, day after day, often extending into the night. In its own way, it was a thorough course. Not contented with this, To'chi's instructor came back the year after the training was finished and gave him further lessons. He had selected a candidate whom he deemed worthy; he was well satisfied with his choice; and he proposed to leave nothing undone. Beyond that point, experience must be the teacher. For thirty-five years, To'chi has been acquiring the knowledge which can come only through experience.

Like most white doctors, To'chi is always on call. Unlike the white doctor, he has no office hours. His practice is carried on in the midst of the ordinary activities of the adult Hopi man. He has his fields which he cultivates, his peach trees from which he gathers and sells the fruit. He helps to take care of his father and mother who are well along in years. And since he has no automobile, he rides horseback to his more distant fields.

If a patient sends for him, he first weighs the circumstances. If, in his judgment, the patient ought to go to the white man's hospital he tells him so.

"The old man up there," he remarked to me one day, "wanted me to do something about his eyes. He is going blind. I told him 'I can give you medicine, but it won't do you any good. You go down to Phoenix to the hospital. They will operate on your eyes. Then you do just what they tell you to do. After that they'll give you glasses and you'll be able to see all right again.'"

"Did he do it?" I asked.

"Oh yes. He's back. He can see now."

He knows that the white doctor can do much that he, as a Hopi doctor, cannot do. "But I can help the white doctor!" he declared.

Hopi Doctor

When someone sends for him from a distance, as often happens, he requires definite assurance that the patient and the patient's family want him to come. Their request cannot be a sudden notion. They must be convinced that he is the one who is needed and that he can succeed, even though others have failed. No doubt he wishes to avoid a needless trip, but I think that, in addition, he desires the patient to have complete confidence in what he can do and that his work shall have the benefit of that confidence.

Those who know about his work do not judge him by the number of cases that come to him but by his success in an individual case. They may make allowance for circumstances which they admit were difficult, but a failure is a failure. He himself would not expect success if he knew that a patient had only partial belief in what he could do, and he has no desire to compromise with himself.

When I called at To'chi's home one time, he had returned not long before from attending a patient in Santa Fe. A member of the family had sent for him several weeks earlier. They knew about him because they themselves were Hopis. For several years, they had been living in Santa Fe, where the father of the family had a job. Now they were desperate because, for the last three years, the father had been unable to work. They did not know the nature of his illness. All that they knew was that he could not work, could not even walk.

To'chi sent back word, asking whether the father himself desired him to come and was confident that he could bring about a cure. He could not undertake treatment unless this was assured. When they replied that all of them wanted him to come, he set out.

What the man was suffering from I do not know. Perhaps

he was in need of mental stimulation, as well as bodily treatment. Perhaps it was wholly a physical illness. At any rate, To'chi remained with the man for three weeks. At the end of that time, his patient was up and around and ready to go back to work. To'chi returned to his own home. Two or three weeks later, he made a return trip to check up on his patient. He found him back at work, putting in full time every day.

I have no knowledge as to the nature of the various illnesses that To'chi has treated. I would not ask a patient, because he would not be able to tell me anything more than his symptoms. I would not ask To'chi himself, because information about a patient's illness is in the province of the doctor, as it is with most white physicians. Perhaps, if I asked about a case, his description would be in different terms from that of a white doctor.

The remedy that To'chi uses is not disclosed to his patient. Probably it would do little more than satisfy his curiosity, and I doubt that it would do even that, for the attitude toward the doctor is one of trusting in measures which are beyond ordinary knowledge. Quite possibly, to disclose the nature of a remedy would result in diminished confidence and would impair the doctor's work. In this, there may be a parallel in the experience of the white doctor.

That To'chi's desert remedies are many and varied is certainly true. That his knowledge of his desert plants is specific and specialized is also true. For him there is a right time and place to collect the coyote sunflower, for example, or one of the many asters, or that plant the Hopis call *kawi'tnga,* which is related to the species from which we get croton oil. Perhaps the right time is in a year following one of more than normal rainfall, perhaps following drouth years. Perhaps, under some conditions or for some purposes, the flower or the seed is gathered, while, under different circumstances, the root might be desirable. These details are specific and obligatory, information that is not likely to be found in textbooks nor in the lexicon of the botanist.

There is reason to suspect that some of the plants that To'chi uses develop more potent properties when growing in the desert than in other environments where moisture favors more luxuriant growth. It is as if the desert sun and aridity distill in the plant a more concentrated essence, along with a smaller stature. The plant, as To'chi collects it, may afford him remedial power which it would not offer in the same degree elsewhere. The guayule plants, it is said, contain a usable concentration of latex when collected in the desert, but a latex content that is too dilute for practical use when raised under irrigation and cultivation. To'chi himself believes that his desert plants are better because of their environment.

No one can question the scientific advantage that the white doctor possesses in the measures which science has provided for him in the last three or four decades—the newer methods of diagnosis through X-rays, and chemical reactions, the synthetic drugs such as the sulfas, and the antibiotics, including penecillin, aureomycin, terramycin, and others. To'chi has the benefit of none of these which we may rightly think of as miracle advances in their capacity to alleviate pain, to correct serious ills, and to prolong life. Nor can he turn to surgery, except to send a patient to a hospital for that purpose. He himself never attempts an operation.

Yet, in his own way and within his unavoidable limitations, he achieves successes. Perhaps these are partially due to his psychological approach to his patient. In any case, the success is real.

Sometimes, his success is won in the face of the preceding failure of others. Last year he was called upon to treat a woman who, for three months, had been under hospital care. She was

KEWAN'VEMA

Of more than usual height, he is strong and erect. He is
in his late seventies or the early eighties. His name,
which is pronounced Keh-wahn'vee-mah, means "Colors painted." Characteristically, he is likely to wear
either a plain white or a plain black bandeau around
his head. The village of Shungopavi, on Second Mesa,
is his home.

suffering from multiple lesions on her arms, legs, and body. The sores were painful, and frightening to see. Out of his stock of desert remedies, To'chi produced a medicine or combination of medicines. Possibly he had treated similar cases before and knew just what to do. At any rate, in three or four days the condition was improved, and at the end of a week the lesions were healed. It may be that the disease was self-limiting and had largely run its course, but if so, I suspect that To'chi's ministrations hastened the cure. It was not likely, I think, to have been wholly coincidental.

The patient who is treated by To'chi is expected to pay for his services, perhaps in money, perhaps in blankets, rugs, or silver. No doubt, this aspect was considered when, as a young man, he entered his training. It is still an important factor today, just as it is with the doctors of our own white race. At the same time, there is sound logic in it regarding the attitude of the patient, his confidence in the man who attends him, and his appreciation of the results achieved. That which you receive free is likely to be too little valued—and this is true for Hopis and Navajos as well as for whites.

To'chi takes his work seriously. Sometimes, when I have been in his home, he has excused himself and started out to visit a patient whom he was attending, perhaps far away. His attitude was one of faithfully meeting a duty. More than once, when I have called at his home, he has been absent on a prolonged case.

And so, a Hopi doctor, To'chi follows the normal life of a Hopi man as much as he can, attending to his own crops and getting in his firewood. In the midst of this work, he practices the healing for which, as a youth, he was trained.

QUA'HU THE EAGLE

A S I WALKED ALONG the village street in the gathering dusk, I
heard overhead a subdued cry that had in it a strange quality of wildness, like a voice from a remote world. Looking up, I
could see on a housetop the form of a tethered eagle, silhouetted
against the darkening sky. The house was that of my friend,
Kel'hoya. The time was the evening before the final ceremony
of the Home Dance, when all of the children and the adults of
the village, gathered in the plaza, would receive gifts at the hands
of the masked dancers, and when Kel'hoya would climb to the
housetop and lay a gift before the captive. On the following day
the fulfillment of destiny, as prescribed by tradition, would come
to the eagle.

It was early in the spring of that year when Kel'hoya, together with Ho'ko, a fellow clansman from another village, set out
from Kel'hoya's home. They had made similar expeditions several times in years past. The earlier trips, thirty or more years
ago, had been made on foot. Later they used a wagon and a team
of mules, but now they started their journey in Kel'hoya's small
truck. A round-about route was required, following available

roads. The latter part of the journey had still to be made by walking and probably climbing.

Their destination was the remote region near White Mesa, where canyons gash the high tableland and no road penetrates. This is the traditional hunting ground for the Snake clan, of which they are members, just as the still more remote region of Navajo Mountain belongs to the Flute clan, the cliffs of Gray Mountain to the Coyotes, the forested slopes of the San Francisco peaks to the Kachina clan, and an area down toward the Little Colorado to the Patki clan.

In the beginning, the story goes, when the clans assembled, they came from various places and directions, some of them from regions a hundred or more miles away, even beyond Marble Canyon and the Vermillion Cliffs, beyond the canyons where the Paiutes now live, beyond the buttes that rise abruptly from the desert in the southeast. These areas were their "home country." By custom, a clan still holds rights in its place of origin, and one of these prerogatives is the right to hunt eagles.

Traditionally, there have been times when a pair of eagles would reward a man for his faithful conduct and his good thoughts by nesting near his village. Kel'hoya and his companion, although they had led good Hopi lives, were not expecting this to happen to them. In forty years it had never taken place. Since they were not expecting it, of course it could not well happen.

The trip which they were now making was preliminary, a scouting expedition. Its purpose was to locate a nest by watching for the parent eagles. At this time the baby eagles would be only a few weeks old, and if they should be taken now, the period during which they would require care would be unnecessarily long, if they survived at all. The best time to secure them is just before

107

they are old enough to use their wings. It is desirable, however, to find an occupied nest in advance and, if possible, to gain some idea when the second trip should be made.

At the end of a hundred miles of driving, the two men left the traveled road and bounced along over the tableland, following a zigzag route which their experience told them would avoid impossible sand and hidden dropoffs. When they were as near their destination as they could manage by car, they drove the car into a clump of junipers, where it might remain hidden from inquisitive Navajos. By now they were in territory beyond the boundaries of the Hopi reservation. From here, they set out on foot, each of them carrying a canteen of water, and one of them a cloth bag containing a dozen of the tough round cakes that the Hopis call *tumoi'viki.*

Following the rough tableland, they made for a promontory from which they could look down into one of the canyons that cut back into the mesa. Here they settled down to watch, talking together when they felt like it and rolling a cigarette from time to time. All about them the mesa and the canyons were steeped in the silence which only the desert can offer. Nothing stirred, not even a rabbit or a lizard.

But luck was with them. Before the sun was halfway to the western horizon they spied a moving speck, high up in the cloudless blue. Almost imperceptibly, it drew nearer, slowly circled, descended, and then disappeared. Picking up the canteens and the bag of *tumoi'viki,* they set out. A mile farther along, they again chose a place on a promontory and again sat down to wait and watch. From this point they commanded two canyons, into one of which the eagle seemingly had descended. Now luck deserted them. The great bird failed to appear again. Perhaps, they said, the eggs are not yet hatched and one of the parent birds is still sitting on the nest. In that case, there would be no frequent, telltale trips to carry food to the young. Perhaps the old eagle was busy securing food but following a course which failed to bring it into view. The thing to do was to wait and see what happened.

When darkness approached they looked about and selected a place where a low-growing juniper sheltered a hollow. In front of this they built a small fire. From the canvas bag came food for their evening meal, and from the canteens tepid but welcome water. In an hour both were asleep.

With the first level rays of the morning sun, they were again on watch. Almost immediately the eagle appeared, seemingly from beneath the promontory on which they had taken their stand. There was no need to conceal themselves; the bird would not abandon its nest. The job now was to find out, if possible, whether there were young birds in the nest or whether the eggs had not yet hatched.

A few yards away the mesa dropped off into the canyon. Standing on the edge, they peered down into the depths, searching the farther canyon wall and as much of the nearer cliff as they could see. Nothing like a nest was in sight.

Lying down flat on a ledge that extended out farthest and seemed to be an overhang, Kel'hoya worked his way out, while Ho'ko held tightly to his feet. "There it is!" Kel'hoya reported. "It's on a shelf about thirty feet down. It must be an old one. There's a big heap of sticks." And then in a few moments, "They're hatched all right! There are two of them."

"Could we climb up from below?" Ho'ko asked.

Kel'hoya studied the situation. "No," he declared. "The nest is on another overhang. There isn't any tree growing near it. When we come back we'll have to get them from here."

The Hopis

"How big are they?" asked Ho'ko.

Again Kel'hoya considered. "They must be two weeks old," he said. "Maybe three."

Back at his own home, each man prepared a number of slender sticks, whittling them smooth. With these he constructed a flat, oblong framework, binding the sticks snugly together where they crossed one another—a small cradleboard. On one side he fastened soft but strong binding material. At one end he contrived a carrying harness. Each prepared, also, a four-foot thong of strong, flexible leather. He cut this in such way that it was wider by a few inches at one end.

Kel'hoya took down a coil of rope from its place on the wall in his home. This he examined thoroughly, inch by inch. It was about a hundred feet long, and Kel'hoya knew that all of this length might be needed. From his son-in-law, who lived in another part of the same house, he obtained also a shorter length, perhaps six feet long.

Before long, Kel'hoya and Ho'ko judged that it was time to make the second trip. They took with them the son-in-law and, in addition, a cousin, Kel'hoya's mother's sister's son, who lived in Ho'ko's village, both of them strong men. No canteens were taken this time, and no bag of *tumoi'viki,* but, in a box, the two cradleboards were carefully stowed, and, with them in the truck body, they took the supply of rope, a burlap bag, a ball of stout twine, and the blunt hammer that Kel'hoya used when laying up a wall. Also, in a small, carefully wrapped parcel, there were four little cakes, made with meal without any added salt.

Once more they crossed the hundred miles to the country of White Mesa and the bumpy tableland to a point as near to the farther promontory as could be managed. There was no need to hide the truck in the midst of junipers this time. They could keep an eye on it; with good luck, they expected not to be absent long anyway. Ten minutes later they stood on the promontory. The two younger men lay down and looked over the edge. "*Lo'-loma!*" they exclaimed. "Good!"

Kel'hoya uncoiled the long rope. At one end he made a snug loop which could not slip and accidentally tighten. The two ends of the short rope he tied together.

As in past years, Kel'hoya planned to make the descent himself. His spare body and light weight made this feasible. Before doing anything further, however, he left the others and walked away to a spot a hundred yards distant. There with the vast canyon before him and the great blue vault of the sky overhead, he made a silent prayer, not for his own safety from accident, but for the success of his venture, for the health and well-being of the young eagles, for their understanding of the mission they were to fulfill and the destiny they were to meet.

The two older men then studied the rock lip of the mesa rim to select the best spot over which to let down the rope and its burden. There was not much choice. No part of the edge was really well rounded.

"This would be a bad job for a horse-hair rope," Ho'ko remarked. "It would cut through. The rope that we have is better."

Eventually they settled on a spot where there was a small groove in the rim. With the blunt hammer which he had brought Kel'hoya worked at this to give it a more rounded contour and to make it smooth, with no rough spots. When this was accomplished to his satisfaction, he and Ho'ko gave their attention to the mesa surface straight back from the rounded groove. At three spots, one behind another, they kicked away earth to uncover crevices in the ledge where the three men who would be stationed there could brace their feet.

III

NUVAM'SA

His name, pronounced Noo-vahm′-sah, means "Snow flakes." Among younger men he is often called by his school name, Peter. Well educated, he has a vigorous mind. His home, which he himself built recently, looks out upon the plaza of Shungopavi. In addition, he is building another home in the outskirts of the village, where he can "have more space" around him when he wishes. In age, he represents the generation whose fathers rank as the oldest men.

Qua'hu the Eagle

Kel'hoya picked up the short rope that he had tied in the form of a small circle. The loop of the long rope he dropped down through this. He slipped the circle over his head and under one arm, so that the long rope was in front of him and near his chest. The burlap bag he fastened under the other arm. Stepping into the loop of the long rope he adjusted it carefully beneath his thighs. Both hands remained free. Ho'ko extended the rest of the long rope straight back, making sure that it could not catch on anything. He and the two younger men took up positions in line, each sitting on the ground with his feet in a crevice, his upper body reclining, his arms extended and the rope firmly grasped. Kel'hoya got down on his hands and knees, facing them while they took up the slack. Then, slowly, he backed over the rim of the cliff.

Little by little, they payed out the rope, while the older man called out instructions. Presently he shouted to them to hold. They could not see what followed, but they knew what was happening. Out there, thirty feet below the rim of the ledge and three hundred feet above the canyon floor, Kel'hoya waited while his body slowly rotated two or three times. The shelf where the nest was built was a long arm's length away because of the overhang. Extending his legs he was able to touch the shelf with a foot and to give himself a push, causing his body to swing out and back like a pendulum. He could almost reach the eagles. Another push and a longer swing. With extended arm, he grasped one of the birds and placed it carefully in the burlap bag. A few moments more, another push—the other bird was secured. The job had not been too difficult; not as bad as the one he had faced one time, when the overhang was greater and the necessary swing much harder to manage. He shouted to the men overhead to haul him up.

The Hopis

Slowly and carefully, a few inches at a time, the three men on top drew the rope toward them. Only one man at a time shifted his hold, the others retaining a secure grasp while he did so. Each man kept both feet solidly placed in his crevice in the ledge.

A few minutes later Kel'hoya, still with the loop under his thighs for security, crawled over the edge. Far off to the west, a growing speck in the sky announced a returning parent eagle, but the men had entertained no fear of trouble on that score. Kel'hoya had uttered his silent prayer. Even if the old eagles had returned sooner, they would have known what the plan was for the young ones, and they would not have attacked him.

Kel'hoya and Ho'ko laid out the cradleboards on the ground. Beside the boards they placed the little cakes that had been made without salt. The spirit of these would sustain and comfort the spirit of the young captives. Each man then placed an eagle on a board, on its back, and bound it gently but firmly in position with its head and its legs free, just as though it were a small child. Using the carrying harness they took the captives to the truck, while the younger men gathered up the ropes and the rest of their equipment. The sun was only an hour or two past *na'shabi,* the middle part of its journey, when they were ready to start back.

"The little bird catches the big bird," mused one of the younger men, as they were driving along. In Hopi language, Kel'hoya means Little Sparrow Hawk.

Arriving home, Kel'hoya set about tethering his eagle. He brought out the leather thong which was wider for a few inches at one end. From his workbox he produced an awl and a length of slender sinew.

Before he freed the little captive from its cradleboard, he fitted the wide end of the thong around one of its legs, just above its spreading foot, and sewed the leather securely. Then, with eagle, cradleboard and thong, he went to the housetop. Up there a perch was waiting, a four-foot length, cut from the limb of a tree and bound at each end to a short and heavier cross log, which in turn was attached by wire to the roof. A board was nailed on one end of the perch for a feeding tray. A heavy staple was driven into the middle of the perch. For a dozen years this arrangement had served the captured eagles. The perch was worn shiny.

Kel'hoya laid the cradleboard on the feeding platform while he attached the free end of the thong to the staple. Then he removed the bandages and permitted the young eagle to do whatever it could in the way of getting up. Although it was still a small bird, its beak and claws were sharp. Kel'hoya climbed down from the roof, went into the house, and cut off a little meat from a rabbit which he had killed the day before. He chopped this up into small pieces and carried them to his captive. Not too much the first day, just enough for a start. Tomorrow there would be more.

Then began, for Kel'hoya, the duty of providing food for his prize, soon in increasing quantities.

"What do you feed it?" I asked.

"Oh, most anything. Squirrel, rabbit. Maybe mice, if I catch any. Sometimes the children bring in mice. But a mouse doesn't go very far. Sometimes it's meat from the store. But it won't do to feed it any birds. If you do that the feathers won't grow as they should. The wing feathers won't be as strong and long as they ought to be, and the downy breast feathers won't be right. You can feed birds to a hawk, but not to an eagle."

By the time the Home Dance ceremony was due, Kel'hoya's eagle had grown to be a strong and vigorous bird. Its plumage was black, with the white tail markings that show when an eagle is in flight. Its talons were large and wicked. Often it spread its wings and hopped a step or two on the perch, but the tough leather thong held. If it had been tethered with a rope, it might have freed itself; if with a chain, it would have caused itself injury. In its own way it seemed to know Kel'hoya. When he brought food to it, he had little need to protect himself except from a chance blow from the wings.

A day or two before the Home Dance, Kel'hoya prepared a present for his eagle. You might have said it was only a little bow and arrow, and so it was. You would have judged, perhaps, that it was a symbol of the chase and therefore appropriate for an eagle. But to Kel'hoya it was more than that and in a way which he could not have expressed in words, for it represented matters that are intangible and indefinable, wishes for well-being and good fortune for the receiver and the giver and for all other persons and beings.

Over in the village to which the other eagle had been taken, Ho'ko also prepared a gift. But his offering was a special kind of Kachina doll, a flat piece of wood painted and decorated in a particular design, for, according to tradition, Ho'ko's eagle was assumed to be a female. When two eaglets are found in one nest, one of them is considered to be a male, the other a female. For the male, the little bow and arrow is the right gift; for the female, the especially designed Kachina. Since Kel'hoya was the leader, as well as the older of the two men, his captive was the male.

On the day of the Home ceremony, while masked figures were carrying stalks of corn and loaves of bread and bundles of cattails into the plaza, while the air still seemed to throb with the beat of a drum and the chant of dancers, Kel'hoya climbed to the housetop and laid his gift before his captive.

Twenty-four hours later destiny came to Kel'hoya's eagle,

not an idle and purposeless end, as Kel'hoya thought of it. Not an end at all, but a beginning.

With a folded blanket over his arm, Kel'hoya climbed once more to the roof. For a few moments he stood there while a wordless prayer took form in his consciousness, a prayer which, in essence, was the same as that which he had offered on the mesa above the eagle's nest, a wish for good fortune and happiness for all creatures. Then he unfolded the blanket and quickly placed it over the eagle. Grasping the captive's body, he pressed his thumb firmly in the little hollow at the base of its neck and held it there. When all struggle had ceased and the eagle was limp in his hands, he removed the blanket and carried the motionless body down to a room in his house.

Two days later Kel'hoya walked alone to a spot outside his village. In his arms he carried the naked body of his eagle. The place to which he went was that which, since time immemorial, has been reserved as the eagle burying ground for members of his clan. Again Kel'hoya spoke a silent prayer as he laid the body of his captive in a crevice in the rocks and covered it with stones.

Back home, Kel'hoya looked over his collection of eagle feathers. There were a half dozen heaps of them on his bed, all carefully sorted. The great pinions lay parallel, one on another, each as long as Kel'hoya's forearm. He picked up one and then another, holding it by its rigid quill and drawing it between his thumb and fingers. Each was a perfect specimen, as springy as thin tempered steel, almost as straight as an arrow. In due time, some of these would find their proper places in the manifold objects required for traditional rites, uses for which no other feathers can qualify.

Next to the pinions lay another group, also straight and

strong but shorter and marked with a white area at the tip, the tail feathers which are spread handsomely when the bird is about to alight. A pair of these, mounted erect on either side of a mask, would look like the alert, inquisitive ears of a hunting animal. Beside these, a collection of much smaller feathers seemed soft on their margins and yet surprisingly strong, the feathers from under the wing. *Kwapi'bhu,* the Hopis call them. Specific functions lay ahead for these. The best of them would decorate the prayer symbols, which are made for the two mythical young men whom the Hopis think of as the grandsons and messengers of the Spider Woman, who is the embodiment of all wisdom.

A great heap of little fluffy feathers was the most important of all. These were the downy breast feathers, symbols of the breath of life. They would fill innumerable functions in Hopi thoughts and prayers. One of them, attached by a slender cotton string to the complicated tassel at the corner of a bride's wedding garment, would symbolize the prayer for a child to be born of her union. On a hundred different types of prayer offerings, a breast feather is needed. One of the little feathers at the end of a very long string serves to indicate the way that guardian spirits are asked to follow. Over one of the round rafters in a Hopi home a little stick is thrust, and from the end of this the fluffy symbol depends, a continuous blessing on those who live within that home.

Thus Qua'hu, the eagle, the bird that rises and soars, up and up, to the very face of Ta'wa, the Sun.

TURTLE

ANYONE WHO HAS WITNESSED one of the major public ceremonies which takes place in a Hopi village plaza must have
been aware of the insistent rhythmic beat of the turtle-shell rattles
worn by the men taking part. It is a distinctive sound,
low-pitched, emphatic, instantly at its maximum as the dancer's
foot strikes the ground, and almost instantly dying away for a
second or two until the beat is repeated. It is a pulsating under-
tone for the high-pitched continuous sound of the gourd rattles
carried by the dancers. With the far-reaching throb of the drum,
it is an effective accompaniment to the deep voices of the dancers,
repeating the traditional chant of the ceremony.

The rattle is attached to the dancer's right leg, just above
the calf. The buckskin thong which holds it in place encircles the
leg like a garter. The turtle shell lies with its longer dimension
crosswise of the leg, its flat undersurface next to the calf. It is
attached only along the upper margin, leaving the body of the
shell free to rise and fall, as if on a hinge. Within the shell there
are two or three dried hooves of antelope or deer which create
the sound.

The rattles worn by individual dancers vary in size from
small ones, as large as a closed fist, to those which are twice as

TAWANIM'PTEWA

His name is derived from Tawa, the sun, and means "Sun covered up." It is pronounced Tah-wah-nim'-pte-wah. No one can say with certainty just how old he is, but he is probably in his late nineties. In any case, he is still very active. His frame is slight, but his muscles are wiry. His white hair, unusual among the Hopis, is worn without a bandeau. His home is in Shungopavi, in one of the older houses, now rebuilt.

large. But whether large or small they rise and fall in unison. The peculiar step of the dancer, raising his right foot a little and bringing it down sharply with the heel striking the ground, gets maximum sound from the hollow shell.

Hova'kpi was not at home when I called at his house one evening. This was not unexpected, for Hopi men have many interests requiring their attention, and Hova'kpi is no exception. Also, the time was mid-summer, and he might have been at work in a distant field somewhere or might have been out herding, or perhaps have gone to the trader's. I asked his sister-in-law, next door, if she could tell me where he might be.

"Oh," she said, "he's gone turtle-hunting."

"What?"

"Turtle-hunting. He left yesterday morning."

The information was mystifying. I could think of no pond or pool in the arid Hopi country big enough or suitable to serve as an adequate home for a turtle family. Red Lake, miles away to the northwest and in Navajo country, was big enough sometimes, but it was only a barren, shallow pond with nothing about it to suggest turtles. Any other pond or pool seemed equally unpropitious and sterile. Perhaps turtle-hunting meant something different from what it would seem to mean. In any case the subject was interesting.

A few days later there was a light in Hova'kpi's window. I knocked on the door, and he called to me to enter. For a few minutes we talked of various matters, but the subject of turtles was uppermost in my mind.

"Your sister-in-law told me that you had gone turtle-hunting," I suggested.

"That's right."

"You mean really hunting turtles?"

"Yes. That's right."

"But where could you go?"

"Well, last year I went down to the Verde River. There's a place down there where I used to get them. It used to be pretty good. But last year it wasn't good any more. I got only two."

I reflected that the Verde River lies south of the great plateau rim. The edge of the rim is one hundred miles or more from Hova'kpi's home, and the river itself would be fifty miles farther, at least.

"This time," Hova'kpi continued, "I went down to the Colorado."

"Way down on the river?"

"That's right. Down below Needles."

That would add another hundred and fifty miles to the journey—Six hundred miles for the round trip. All for the sake of securing some turtles.

Little by little the story came out, part of it at this visit, part in later conversations.

One day in early summer Ko'ko and Ta'bo, fellow clansmen from another village, drove over to call on Hova'kpi, riding in Ko'ko's pickup truck. They proposed a trip to hunt for turtles. Neither of them had ever made such an expedition, whereas Hova'kpi had made many and knew all about it. Ko'ko would furnish the transportation, and Ta'bo would buy the gas. Each of the three would keep whatever turtles he could catch. They agreed to start the day after the *Niman* ceremony in Hova'kpi's village. This would be convenient because the two men would come over to the village anyway to see the ceremony. Hova'kpi said that they would have to start early because the drive would be a long one.

126

Turtle

The afternoon of the ceremony, when the dancers had nearly finished their last appearance, the three men visited the trading post. Each of them bought a can or two of tomatoes and such other provisions as he fancied. Jointly, they bought a large watermelon, since the melons in their own gardens were not yet ripe. Hova'kpi added a small bag of wheat flour. "That's for the turtles," he said. A cardboard carton held the provisions. "That will be for turtles, too," Hova'kpi suggested. Ko'ko and Ta'bo filled up the gas tank of the truck.

At Hova'kpi's house, they carried the carton inside, where it would be safe for the night. "Too many Navajos around," Ta'bo remarked. Hova'kpi brought out a stout knife with a slender, keen blade, six or seven inches long, and stowed it in the carton, along with a ball of stout cord. After they had prepared and eaten supper, they packed a coffeepot, frying pan, stew pan, and cups, in a small box, ready for the trip. With a thoughtful look in his eye, Hova'kpi took down a coil of rope from the wall and added it to their equipment. Then he arranged rugs and sheepskins on the floor for his guests.

Their start the next morning was made soon after sunrise. A quick breakfast of hot coffee and *tumoi'viki,* and they were on their way. The western escarpment of the mesa was still in shadow as they descended to the vast country down below. Half an hour later they laid aside the coats that they had been wearing because of the early morning desert crispness. In another two hours they had crossed the Little Colorado.

In Flagstaff they stopped, because Ko'ko and Ta'bo had decided that they would take with them another loaf of store bread. Then they stopped again, because Ko'ko spied a Navajo who owed him a balance on a bracelet and suggested that they wait while he collected or, at any rate, induced the Navajo to

127

make a payment on the debt. This last stop took an hour, but the other two men were not impatient, for they wanted Ko'ko to succeed. A Navajo is useful, but he needs to pay up now and then.

At Williams, they stopped to visit a store where Hova'kpi had purchased, last year, a pound of rough turquoise which had turned out well on grinding. He wished to see what further stock might be available and ask the price. All three men, well acquainted with turquoise, looked over the available material. Some of it, they agreed, was rich in color and ought to work up into good settings for rings or bracelets, but their comments to that effect were in Hopi which the storekeeper did not speak. As noontime had come and gone, they remained in Williams for lunch.

They went on, then, toward the west, following the highway which would take them through rugged country where hills and mountains lie on either side, on down the long descent toward Kingman and the further descent to the Colorado.

The afternoon was waning. As the sun was going down they found an acceptable spot not far from the road and made camp. Hova'kpi knew that they would need daylight to make their way to the river and select a place where a slough or a back water offered promising hunting. Before going to bed, Hova'kpi dumped two or three cupfuls of flour into the stew pan and added water slowly from his canteen, stirring the mixture until it was a thick, doughy mass.

By the time the sun had risen they were again on their way. A back road and a trail which a truck could negotiate carried them to a place where they were able to establish a base camp, with a quiet stretch of water in sight a half-mile beyond. "Not so many mosquitoes here," Hova'kpi explained. "Better place to sleep." With no other human beings likely to be in sight, whatever possessions they might leave in the truck would be safe.

A few willows were growing near by. Hova'kpi looked them over and selected one with a straight, slender stem an inch or so in diameter. He cut this off and prepared a length of about three feet, sharpening each end to a point. His companions did the same. Then, with the coil of rope over his shoulder, and carrying the ball of cord and the pan in which he had mixed flour and water, he led the way to the river's bank.

They all stripped to the bare skin. Knowing that Ko'ko could swim only a little, and Ta'bo not at all, Hova'kpi waded in while the others waited. He found the water four or five feet deep for a distance of several yards from the bank, but dropping off then three or four feet more. Swimming and wading, he established a rough line beyond which Ta'bo could not safely go.

Returning to the bank, he tied his sharpened stick across his chest, fastening it securely. On each of the pointed ends he stuck a small ball of dough, tying it so that it could not easily slip off. Ko'ko and Ta'bo followed his example. Hova'kpi waded in while the others watched. When he was in water up to his shoulders he took a deep breath and disappeared beneath the surface, remaining submerged for a long minute. When he came up he explained the technique to his companions.

"You stay under as long as you can," he said. "You move along right down next to the bottom. If you can, you crawl along the bottom. If there's a turtle anywhere near, he'll come over to see what's going on. But you must go slow so as not to scare him. After a while he'll want to get some of the dough. Just as soon as he begins to nibble you bring your arm around and grab him."

"Can you always get him?" Ta'bo questioned.

Hova'kpi laughed. "No," he said. "He's likely to get away.

Sometimes you can catch him, but you have to be pretty quick. If you miss him he won't come near any more for a while. You have to keep on until he's willing to come back or until some other turtle comes along. You've got to be quiet and go slow, or there won't be any come to the bait." He cautioned Ta'bo. "Don't go out too far," he said. "When you crawl along, work toward the bank where it gets shallower."

All three set to work, then, Hova'kpi going out to deeper water. When noon came, Hova'kpi had caught two turtles, Ko'ko one. The captives were placed in the cardboard carton, and the top was weighted with a log. Out on the bank, they prepared lunch, with half of the watermelon to top it off, and loafed for an hour. In the afternoon Hova'kpi caught two more, and Ko'ko again one, but Ta'bo was empty-handed. "I've had a couple of nibbles," he complained, "but they got away."

An hour before sunset, Hova'kpi said that it was time to stop and take care of the turtles that they had caught. "It takes time to do that," he explained. They dressed and carried their carton to the camping place, leaving on the bank their pointed sticks and the coil of rope, but taking with them the unused part of the ball of cord.

Back at the truck, Hova'kpi cut off two short lengths of the cord and tied a slip-knot in one end of each. He fished out one of the turtles from the carton and told Ko'ko to hold it securely by the margin of the shell. In a few minutes the turtle slowly extended a foot. Watching for this, Hova'kpi slipped a noose over the foot and drew it tight. Presently the captive extended a foot on the other side, and again Hova'kpi slipped a noose over it.

"We'll need these," he explained, "to help us clean out the shell."

Turtle

Under Hova'kpi's instructions, Ko'ko placed the turtle on the ground on its back. Ta'bo took one cord, Ko'ko the other, and both pulled hard. Hova'kpi waited with the slender, keen knife. When the turtle extended its head, he thrust the blade into the base of its neck and deep into its body. There was a struggle for a few moments, which gradually diminished and before long was at an end.

Then came the task of cutting the body away from the inside of the shell and removing it. This was not an easy job, nor could it be hurried. The muscles were tough and their attachment to the shell was like horn. The shell itself must not be marred outside nor gouged inside. A long half-hour was required for the work. When it was finished, the three men inspected the prize, admiring the large irregular markings on the well-arched convex back and the smooth surface of the under side.

The work on two more turtles was completed before dark. After supper, the remaining two were finished by the light of a small fire of dry willow sticks. Before they went to bed, Hova'kpi proposed that they remain for another day's hunting. "We have five turtles," he said, "and that is good. But Ta'bo hasn't any. There are more in the river where we have been hunting. Maybe some more will be coming there because they have smelled the bait. We can hunt tomorrow, and if we start early the next day we can get home that night." The other two agreed.

By midafternoon of the following day, Hova'kpi, more experienced and able to range farther because he was a good swimmer, had brought in three more. Ko'ko and Ta'bo were out of luck. Ta'bo worked steadily while the other two men sat on the bank and smoked a cigarette. Hova'kpi, watching closely, saw Ta'bo come up with a turtle in the crook of his right arm, his left hand helping to hold it as it tried to get away. He was close

SIKIES'TEWA

The oldest of the living grandsons of the famous Tuba, he lives just south of the village of Kiakochmovi, in the valley below Old Oraibi, where he was born eighty-nine years ago. His name is pronounced See-kai-es'-tee-wah, and means "Yellow settled down." Both his home and his crop lands are maintained with diligent care.

to the place where deeper water began, and the next moment began to slip down the sloping bottom. In a dozen fast strokes, Hova′kpi had reached him and was helping him back to shallower water. They climbed out, Ta′bo still holding tight to his prize.

As the three men made ready to go back to their camping place, Hova′kpi picked up the coil of rope and slung it over his shoulder. "We didn't need it after all," he remarked, "but it was best to have it along."

Once more they worked by the light of a fire to finish the task of cleaning the day's lot of turtle shells. There were ten now, seven of them caught by Hova′kpi, two by Ko′ko, and one by Ta′bo. Two of those that Hova′kpi had captured were large shells, at least eight inches long. The rest were all of medium size. "It's a good place for turtles," Hova′kpi remarked. "Next time we make a trip Ta′bo will get more."

Their journey home the next day was begun when there was only a faint glow of light in the east. "It's different going back," said Ko′ko. "We know just where we're going to be tonight, and it doesn't make any difference if we're late. We ought to make it by eight o'clock, maybe by seven, if we don't stop too much."

They drove first to Hova′kpi's home before going on to the other village. He suggested that they leave their turtle shells with him for a few days. He would go over each shell once more to make sure that no bit of flesh was left inside. Since he had the right kind of long, slender knife, he could do this better than they.

When I visited Hova′kpi, just after his turtle hunt, and he told me what he had been doing, my questions must have reflected my interest. Before I left he went into an adjoining room and came back with the carton of turtle shells.

"Seven of them are mine," he explained. "The other three belong to my friends."

"What will you do with them?" I asked.

He picked out a shell of medium size, easily identifying it by details of its markings. "This one," he said, "belongs to Ta'bo. He's going to keep it for himself because the one he has is not very good any more. Ko'ko is going to give one of his to his uncle and keep the other one. I have a nice one already, so I'll sell mine to men who need them."

He took one of the large ones from the carton and examined it critically. "That's a pretty good shell," he said. "It will make a fine rattle. Somebody will want it who hasn't a good one. He'll give eight dollars for it. The smaller ones will bring four dollars each. They're good shells."

Thoughtlessly I said that I would like to make a picture of them. Hova'kpi spoke gently in his reply. "I'm sorry," he said, "but you know they're to use in ceremonies. It wouldn't be right to make a picture. I think you'll understand."

WHEN THE SUN TURNS

MIDAFTERNOON SUNLIGHT of an early December day slanted across the gray rock plateau of First Mesa. In Walpi it bathed in crystal warmth the compact houses that look out upon Wepo Wash. On the opposite side the passage leading out of the constricted plaza was shadowy cool. In Sichomovi, the plaza margin, where in August a narrow band of shade offered grateful advantage to those who watched the closing measures of the *Niman* ceremony, now stood empty beneath the cloudless blue of the unfathomable sky. On the sunlit side of the plaza a venerable Hopi was seated on the low stone bench, spinning cotton string. His hand moved smoothly over the spinning stick which lay across his leg, while the cotton was transformed from a fluffy white strand into a smooth and closely twisted cord.

Siva'pi and I drew near to watch his work and to pass the time of day. My companion and the older man talked together in Hopi.

"He says that he has already finished two balls of string," Siva'pi interpreted. "It's for the *Soya'la*. That will begin in a few days now, and you must have cotton string for the prayer offerings."

We walked along and knocked on the door of Ba'toti, another of the older Hopis. When he called to us to enter we stepped into the one-room house where he lives alone. He really is an old man, past ninety, and shows his age by the short and uncertain steps that he takes when walking. Although he no longer has anyone sharing his home, he is looked after by members of his family, who keep him supplied with water for his big earthen jar and fuel for his small stove, and who provide a place for him at their meals.

When we walked into his house he was carding cotton. Now he resumed his task while he talked with Siva'pi. He was seated on a low wooden stool, no more than eight or ten inches high. His supply of cotton was on a mat beside him. As he worked at the fibres with his two cards, the cotton took shape in a soft, white strand, a few inches long and an inch in diameter. When a strand was completely satisfactory, he laid it beside its fellows on the mat.

"He says that this is the last of the carding," Siva'pi explained. "He has most of his spinning done, too, and will finish it tomorrow."

As the afternoon drew to a close, we walked over to a place near the house on the top of which the Sun Watcher was seated. From that point he could observe the spot on the western horizon where the setting sun touched the distant mountains. Three weeks ago the point of contact had been high up on the San Francisco peaks. Daily it had moved to the left, down the long slope, until now, as December unrolled, it approached the place where the descending slope disappeared behind an intervening mesa.

"It will arrive down there," said Siva'pi, "in three or four days. When it gets there the Sun Watcher will report to the chiefs in the Chief Kiva. Then they will decide when the Soya'la will begin. There is another place, too, for watching the sun. It's out on the end of the mesa, beyond the last house. There is a little

138

hollow in the ledge where a man can sit, and there are notches in the ledge in front of him. But it's the sunrise that you watch from there, not the sunset. Sometimes the Sun Watcher has an assistant. One of them watches the sunrise from the hollow in the ledge, and the other watches the sunset. Then they compare notes to make sure that they are right."

Visiting with Siva'pi that evening, I asked him to tell me what he could about the significance of the *Soya'la,* the great ceremony in which the Hopi people celebrate the winter solstice, the day when the sun begins to return from its farthest southern point. I knew that many details of the ceremony he could not discuss with me or with anyone other than a Hopi. But the part that takes place outside the kivas anyone can see. I wanted to know whatever I might be allowed to know concerning those aspects, and I wanted to understand the Hopi thoughts about the season that the *Soya'la* celebrates.

Of all the Hopi ceremonies, the *Soya'la* is perhaps the most fundamental and far-reaching. It is more than a petition for rain or for successful crops; more than the supplication for rebirth, which is symbolized by the ceremony of the New Fire; more than the prayer for a true coming-of-age and for long life, as enacted in the *Wu'wuchim.* These relate primarily to the active participants in the ceremony, to their households and the spectators. The *Soya'la* is directed toward everyone, far and near—in essence, toward all mankind, both the living and the dead. It includes in its prayers all creatures, all plants, and all things which touch upon human life. It embodies an all-inclusive wish for well-being.

The *Soya'la* is celebrated at the time of the winter solstice, because the return of the sun symbolizes the beginning of a new period of life and growth, and therefore a renewal of all that human beings need and desire. Without that return, there could be no

139

life on earth, no plants, no animals, no human beings. In Hopi beliefs it is fitting that the prayers for human welfare should go forth as the sun begins its life-giving return. It is proper that this should be a time of rejoicing, when good wishes go out to everyone everywhere.

Since the ceremony is timed to the winter solstice, it often is referred to by the Hopis as *Ta'wa A'hoyi*, which means "The Sun Turns Back." The name *Soya'la* is a shortened form of *Soya'luna* which may be translated as "They come out." The reference is to the Kachinas, beloved spiritual concepts of the Hopis', who begin their return with the enactment of this ceremony. For six months they have been absent in what the Hopis think of as their home. Now the first of them, impersonated by a ceremonial figure and his two sisters, who enact a brief symbolic drama, return to the daily life of the people whom they guard and instruct.

In one way or another, every household shares in the ceremony. All adult men participate, because all take part in the fashioning of the traditional prayer offerings and their distribution. All youths who have passed their initiation take part in like degree. This includes a considerable number, for the reason that every young man becomes in due course a member of one of the four tribal societies, the Singers, the Agaves, the Horns, or the *Wu'wuchim*. Initiation takes place usually when a boy is in his teens. After he has completed his initiation, he is entitled to participate in kiva activities, and therefore can join other men in the enactment of the *Soya'la*. Through the program as it develops, the women of Hopi households are brought into the drama. Thus, to an impressive degree, this ceremony represents a marked breadth of active participation on the part of the Hopi people, which is in keeping with the universal scope of its objectives.

When the Sun Turns

Specific injunctions are laid upon every household during the time that the *Soya'la* is in progress, from its first beginning to its final act. Everything must be left "as it was created by the Great Power." Nothing may be destroyed. No animal, large or small, may be killed or harmed. Although costumes are assumed and decorations laid on, there must be no cutting of hair. Furthermore, the Hopi fixed custom requiring that you knock on a door before entering some one's house is now reversed. If you enter you must do so without knocking.

Since in certain years several societies may be responsible for special parts of the ceremony, the representatives of those societies may, in those years, perform as specific actors in the drama. Thus many men have an additional participation beyond that of fashioning prayer offerings. They have creative roles, through which they contribute to the whole complex picture.

In accordance with tradition, the direction of the ceremony as it is enacted on First Mesa lies with the Patki clan. The chief of the clan is chief of the ceremony. The Sun Watcher is a prominent member of the clan. These responsibilities are taken seriously, and the positions are held in honor. The returning Kachinas —*Au'halani* and his two sisters—are enacted by Patki members. The original home of the Patki clan is thought to be a region to the south, from which important ceremonial objects were derived. That region is thought of also as the home of the clouds, which often represent both human and supernatural spirits.

A few days after Siva'pi and I had visited Ba'toti and watched him card cotton, the Sun Watcher was ready to report to the leaders. Four days earlier the setting sun had reached the notch in the mountain horizon. Therefore, the traditional time for announcement had arrived. The leaders were assembled in the "house" of the Patki clan, the place where objects that are

SIWIQUAP'TEWA

He is almost universally known by the name of Seba James. His Hopi name, pronounced See-wee-quap'-tee-wah, means "Small plant that has taken hold." He lives in the border of the village of Kiakochmovi, usually called New Oraibi, and is a skilled grower of fruits, vegetables, and farm crops. An occasional White delegation comes to see and admire the fruits that he grows. His age is about seventy-five, or perhaps a year or two more.

sacred to the clan are kept. There the Sun Watcher joined them to take his part in their preliminary ceremony.

Early the next morning, in the dim light before the sun had risen, the Crier chief, Chaa'kmonwi, made his way to the top of the highest house to scatter sacred meal, toward the east, north, west, and south, up toward the zenith, and down toward the nadir. Returning to the clan "house," he waited a few moments. Then as the sun began to appear above the far-off horizon his voice carried his message to the silent houses on the mesa, like the ringing of an early morning bell. On the fourth day from now, he said, the *Soya'la* would begin.

The white visitor on First Mesa might understandably have wished that, four days later, he could witness the drama then beginning in the Chief Kiva, to see the details of the ceremony which for several days would be unfolding. This of course could not be possible, since this ancient drama is for the Hopis alone. It is fundamentally religious in character and cannot be open to a public who would not be able to participate. But there are aspects of it which are enacted in the open. Through these and through their symbolism, the visitor may gain some understanding of the significance attached to the details of the ceremony.

At sunrise on this first day a standard, called the *Soya'la na'chi,* was set up above the hatchway entrance to the Chief Kiva to indicate that sacred activities were now beginning within and that only those who were entitled to do so might enter. Similar standards were placed above other kivas. Each was a two-foot stick, painted black and bearing at one end two prominent feathers from the tail of the red-shafted woodpecker. These symbols remained in position throughout the progress of the ceremony.

At noon one of the leaders emerged from the Chief Kiva,

carrying four prayer sticks bound to a willow staff. One of these represented an ear of corn, to which downy feathers were attached by a cotton string. Each of the other three was a double prayer stick of the design especially identified with the *Soya'la*. The messenger made his way down from the mesa to a spring which to the Hopis is sacred and which is called *Tawa'pa,* the Sun Spring. Wading into the water, he deposited his offering beneath the surface, thrusting it down so that it remained immersed. Thus the leaders symbolized their prayer to the spirit of the sun and their exhortation for the return of its life-giving warmth.

In the evening of this same day, the return of the Kachinas was celebrated by the appearance of the figures called Au'halani, the Elder Brother, and his two sisters, Yellow Corn Girl and Blue Corn Girl. After first enacting a secret ritual in the Chief Kiva, they visited each of the other kivas on the mesa. All three figures were masked. Au'halani wore a ceremonial kilt and sash. A white stripe was painted down each leg and arm. His mask covered his head. The face of the mask was painted green. A green and black horn projected from one side of the mask, a short fan from the other. In one hand he carried a staff decorated with turkey feathers near the base, with an ear of corn near the top, and in the other hand a flat "chief's stick," on which an ear of corn was carved in low relief. The two female figures who accompanied him also wore kilts, and, around the upper body, white woolen blankets with blue and red borders.

The leaders, once they had entered the Chief Kiva, remained there until the major part of the entire ceremony was concluded. During this time, Siva'pi explained, they are not a part of their own households. From the beginning they fast. Their only food is a fragment of a special wafer bread which is made without salt and prepared by certain women who are entitled to make it.

146

When the Sun Turns

A tiny piece of this is given to each one in the kiva to make his body right and good. It is a symbolic food, intended for the spirit as well as the body.

During the next two days, more and more men made their way to the various kivas, carrying with them supplies which they would need in fashioning prayer offerings. Each man joined other members of his clan in whatever kiva the clan owned or occupied for this occasion. To the visitor on the mesa came the sound of songs which the men in the kivas were singing. "These are *Soya'l* songs," Siva'pi explained to me later. "They are sung because this is the time when the sun is soon to start his return journey. They ask the sun not to forget the people who wait for him. They wish for new life and happiness for everyone. All the men in the kivas are busy while they are singing. They are getting ready for the important part that will come in another day."

That day, the most significant in the series, began long before dawn with a ritual timed to the setting of the constellation Orion. Then soon after sunrise all of the men who were participating in the ceremony went to their own homes for the preparatory rite, in which the hair is washed in suds made with the root of the narrow-leaved yucca. By this means, each man was purified in order that he might make the prayer offerings which would occupy his activities during the rest of the day. From that time on, for the remainder of the day, all were in the kivas.

The offerings which they made were of many kinds, depending on the objective to which the offering was directed— the happiness of an individual person, a blessing on a house, the health and strength of a domestic animal, the fruition of crops, or any one of many other desired ends. Each offering, however, no matter what its objective was, made use of one or another bird

147

feather. "These are used," said Siva'pi, "because some feathers are like the clouds, and the clouds are like the spirits. The downy feathers are like the breath. They represent what you would call the soul. Sometimes they come from the breast of an eagle, sometimes from the turkey. In a prayer offering for rain, it is right to use the feathers of a duck. In a prayer for a good crop of peaches, we use the breast feathers of the owl and the yellowbird because these belong with warm weather. For horses, it is right to use many feathers tied together. But most important of all is the little downy breast feather attached to a piece of cotton string because that is always the breath of life.

"The stick to which a feather is attached is significant, too. If it is for a blessing on a house, it can be a little willow twig, or one from a shrub that has downy leaves. If it is a prayer to the clouds, it can be a long slender branch with a feather from the yellowbird on the end. If it is for cattle or sheep, it will be in the form of a small cross because the ends on each side represent the ears. The antelope prayerstick is flat and bears marks which are like an inverted V, resembling the footprints of an antelope. The eagle-egg prayer offering is made of cottonwood painted white and marked with black spots. The *Soya'l* prayerstick is double, representing male and female. It has a turkey feather back of it to symbolize a blanket, and it has a twig of sage and a sprig of the plant which we call *bam'navi*. Every prayer offering, except the one for peaches, has a triple needle of pine. That is not used for peaches because it would bring cold. Always a little piece of corn husk is attached to a prayer offering. Inside of this there is some meal and a little honey. This represents food for the prayer while it is on its way so that it may have strength and be sure to reach its destination."

Later Siva'pi pointed out four prayer offerings of a different kind which had been deposited in a shrine. Each of these was a slender stick, the upper part of which was curved over like a crook. From the tip of each hung a cotton string with a downy feather at the end. There were four sizes of these, from small to large. They represent old persons with heads bowed toward the ground. When you visit the shrine you touch first the largest one and pray that you also may live to be old. Then you touch the next one and the next, and last of all the smallest, which signifies a person who is very old indeed, and you pray that you also may continue in life to a very old age.

In the afternoon of the day devoted to the making of prayer offerings, two of the men in the Chief Kiva came out bearing an empty basket. With this they began making the rounds of the principal houses. At each home the woman of the household was waiting for them with two or three ears of corn tied together with yucca. She placed the bundle in the basket. When it was full the messengers carried it into the Chief Kiva.

As the sun was setting all the men came out from the kivas to distribute prayer offerings to friends and relatives. Many of the men already wore downy feathers thrust into their hair. They walked in groups according to their clan membership. When a man met another and presented him with a prayer offering he greeted him with a Hopi phrase meaning "May you, my friend, have every happiness that you desire." A similar phrase was used in presenting an offering to a woman. No one was forgotten. It was like the white man's Christmas or New Year, but with gifts signifying well-being and happiness rather than the presents to which we are accustomed.

Many of the prayer offerings made in the various kivas were carried to the Chief Kiva, to remain there through the night and, thus, to receive the blessing which would be given them by the

149

rites that would take place there in the course of the evening and night. These rites constitute, probably, the heart of the entire ceremony, the most significant part of the ancient ritual. In some years a prolonged and colorful drama, performed by members of the tribal societies, occupies most of the night. This is in addition to traditional rites enacted by individuals. In order that I might have some understanding of the scope of this program and its symbolism, Siva'pi told me a little about it. He was careful not to describe details and not to violate the reserve that all Hopis feel in connection with their ancient rituals.

The performances, which are given by representatives of the tribal societies, dramatize the return of the sun and the phenomena which that return makes possible. The participants prepare for their part in their own kivas and enter the Chief Kiva to enact the successive steps of the drama, including the return of birds, the coming of clouds and rain, the return of longer days, the coming of the Kachinas, the disappearance of ice and snow, the reappearance of crops, and the commanding role of the sun.

The men of the Horns Society, decked with many downy feathers on head and body, impersonate the returning birds. In the next act, performed by the Singers, a magnificent shield, three or four feet in diameter and set all around with great eagle pinions, makes its appearance. In the center, a painting depicts clouds and rain. A similar shield with the morning star in the center is carried by the representative of the *Wu'wuchim* society, which presents the third act. This is followed by a performer who carries a shield with an antelope in its center, and this in turn by Horn men whose shield carries a painting of a Kachina identified with a spirit home in ice caves. The Agaves now enter carrying a shield depicting snow and hail. Another follows, displaying a shield bearing a Kachina decked with a girdle of corn ears. And finally the *Wu'wuchim* men close the series with a great sun shield.

An individual drama is enacted by the Hawk youth, *Ki'sha Ti'yo,* and his companion the Hawk maiden, *Ki'sha Ma'na.* This is performed, in part, in the open. The youth is costumed with a brightly-colored, feather headdress. His chin is blackened, and so are his feet. The maiden carries a framework of crossed rods which are arranged to represent clouds. This is decorated with a squash blossom at each intersection. As Siva'pi pointed out, the blossoms are beautifully contrived by a means which only the makers know how to produce and are handsomely dyed. After a long ritual, the youth and the maiden dance together. In the course of the dance the maiden shakes the frame which she carries and dislodges the squash blossoms. The dance and other details of the drama symbolize the rebirth of all plants and all creatures —the new life that is now to begin.

In another individual act, a man wearing on each arm eagle feathers, which extend from shoulder to wrist, performs an ancient dance, symbolic of the great bird that he impersonates. In still another performance, a man who carries a decorated staff and other symbolic objects takes the part of a cloud.

When the long day and night of ritual were ended, sunrise found the men from all the kivas emerging to distribute their prayer offerings, some to homes, some to shrines and springs, others to horses and burros, cattle, sheep and farms—to all the varied objectives for which the offerings were fashioned. One of the leaders emerged from the Chief Kiva, spread a cloth on the ledge near by, and returned down the ladder. In a few moments, he and others came out bearing the bundles of corn ears which had been collected the preceding day from the various households and which had been near the altar throughout the

PAWI'KI

To many, especially to his White friends, he is known as Sam. Quick in his movements, he has a mobile face and an equally nimble mind. His activity belies his eighty-odd years. His home is in Kiakochmovi. Like many others of this village, he was born in Old Oraibi. His name, pronounced Pah-wee'-kee, means "Duck."

most important part of the ceremony. These were placed on the cloth. Soon the women of the households came to select and take home their own bundles. Each carried her bundle to the store-house of her home and placed it on top of the seed corn for the coming year, that it might convey to the other seeds the consecration which it had received while in the Chief Kiva. When planting time arrived, these special ears would be the first to enter the ground and would prepare the way for the bountiful crop that all Hopis pray for and need.

Thus, for the people of First Mesa, the *Soya'la* came to an end.

In an epilogue the following day, the leaders assembled in the house of the Sun Chief. From mid-morning to midafternoon they worked at fashioning the offerings called Sun prayer sticks or in Hopi *Ta wa pa'hola la'uwa,* made from stems of the blue willow and bearing four breath feathers. At dawn the next morning their offerings were taken from the Sun Chief house to the Chief Kiva, where the leaders assembled. All of the prayer sticks were placed in a white blanket. Carrying this, a messenger set out for an altar four miles to the east, the Sun House. There he deposited them, one by one, facing the east, where the rising sun could shine upon them.

MAN AND MYSTIC

"Y̶ou know," said a Hopi friend, a man of keen mind and broad views, "the Hopis are a very religious people."

The reaction of the white man to this statement will be strongly influenced by various factors. If his impressions are derived from a newspaper account of a Snake Dance in which the only matter stressed is the carrying of a snake in the participant's mouth, he will no doubt think of these people as barbaric and will be loath to concede to them anything which he is willing to accept as religious in his definition of the term. If he is a chance visitor who has spent a day driving through the reservation he may feel that he has witnessed nothing suggesting a religious interest, especially since the only church buildings that he has seen are three or four small chapels belonging to Christian missions. If he is a devout member of a Christian faith and has been told by some one that the Hopis worship the sun, he may declare that such worship is paganism, not religion in any true sense. If he chances to see a public ceremony in a village plaza, he may declare that while it is colorful it cannot be considered more than a curious pageant characterized by unintelligible sounds and outlandish costumes.

Man and Mystic

Nevertheless, if you know the Hopis more than superficially, if you are willing to think of religion in terms other than those in which you were brought up, you will agree with my Hopi friend. Furthermore, as you come to perceive some of the foundations of those beliefs, the earnestness with which they are held, and the extent to which they pervade daily life, you may conclude that the Hopi people are in fact remarkably religious.

There is never, I think, a time of day or an occasion in which a Hopi fails to feel some influence of his beliefs. He may violate some admonition, may be guilty of an act which his tenets condemn—for after all he is as human as we are—but his religion is with him more continually and forcefully than is the case with many of us of the white race. From childhood, his pattern of conduct is set before him as something whole and indivisible. A part of the pattern may become lost for a time in the stress of existence and conflicts, or may be overlaid by the colors of emotion, but, as a pattern, it is not consciously trimmed or modified. A Hopi does not say, "This part may be all right for others but not for me."

The body of Hopi beliefs cannot be explicitly defined and catalogued, as those of many other religions have been. Since they have had no written language of their own, there has been for them no possibility of setting down a statement of their precepts of conduct and expositions of philosophy. The declarations of the Koran or the Analects of Confucius could have no counterpart, even in small degree, because, no matter how wise a Hopi leader might be, he can do no more than pass along his wisdom in his spoken counsels. No comparison can be made with the beliefs of the present-day Christian faiths, because the latter have had many years in which their various creeds have become differentiated, crystallized, and defined. With the Hopis, beliefs must be inferred.

The Hopis

In conversation with Hopi friends you do not find them stating a creed or defining beliefs. A specific rule of conduct may emerge, especially if an unwritten rule has been violated. If some one steals, the fact will clearly develop that stealing is wrong and is never to be condoned. This principle is firmly and explicitly held. It applies to everyone, whether Hopi, Navajo, or white; there are no exceptions. In the same way deliberate falsehood is condemned. If a man indulges in it for the sake of gain or to protect himself from a deserved penalty, he violates an unchangeable rule. Another rule is broken if a son fails to provide that which an aged parent needs and cannot provide for himself. These and others are accepted principles of right living, but no one assembles them and sets them down as a code. Similarly, the Hopi views as to the relation of human life to the surrounding world, the power of prayer, the influence of thoughts, whether good or bad, the existence of a life hereafter, the validity of dreams, the possibility of revelations, and the importance of undivided allegiance to a spiritual concept—these are set forth in no declaration. They are of vital significance in Hopi life, but they are implicit, not specifically defined.

The foundation of Hopi views is a firm belief in an active and significant spirit world which is coexistent with the physical world and is always to be taken into account in the activities of a man's life. This spirit world encompasses all human beings. It includes lesser animals, especially those which in any way touch upon human existence. In a more limited degree it involves plant life, particularly the crops essential for food. In a different manner and with reservations it may include natural phenomena, such as clouds or rain, and the important celestial bodies.

As for human beings, the Hopi belief in a spirit world is closely akin to that of all men everywhere. Such a belief, of course, is the foundation of all religions, including Christianity. The Hopi view differs somewhat, because it holds that the spirit of one who has died may at times be thought of as part of a great, indefinable world which is both the source of all spirits and the place to which they return and with which they may be merged—this is believed in spite of the fact that the individual human being is also thought of as retaining his specific identity after leaving this life. These two concepts seem not to conflict in the Hopi mind but to be mutually flexible and to adjust themselves in accordance with circumstances.

Among the Hopis there is no setting out to prove the existence of a world encompassing all human spirits, past and present, and no thought of such a procedure. It simply is accepted as such a universal human experience that it is completely convincing in and by itself, needing no proof. Apparently there is no part of Hopi society which needs assurance, since all have grown up in the presence of the universally held concept. Perhaps, if you were to ask for proof, they would ask you in turn how you would undertake to demonstrate with physical means that which is not physical.

Regarding animals, the belief in a spirit representing a certain animal is firmly held when there is occasion to bring it to mind, but is not continually in thoughts. It does not have the universal significance characteristic of the belief in a human spirit. Different animals are likely to be in the forefront at different times, such as those which play a prominent part in ceremonies and those which appear in Hopi myths. Since there are many desert animals which fall within these two classifications—bears, for example, coyotes, badgers, hawks, eagles, snakes, beetles, butterflies, and numerous others—it follows that the realm of the spirit world that is concerned with animals is very large.

The Hopis

A place in the spirit world for animals is essential, and the possession of definite personalities is logical. The belief concerning them is deeper than the feeling which most of us have toward a pet animal whose reactions to us seem beyond and above the purely physical and give the impression of a responsive and understanding personality.

A Hopi is firm in the belief that an animal, through its spirit, is aware of the attitude and intentions of a human being. Although an animal has no common language with man, it responds to an unspoken message and understands. Although it may be a creature which normally would fear man, or one which is capable of doing him harm, it is instructed and led by the spirit of man, which is imparted to its own spirit.

I was talking one day with two men whom I chanced to run across, neither of whom I had known before. The conversation turned to the snakes used in the Snake Ceremony. One of the two, a man of especially matter-of-fact manner, expressed his views in direct and unequivocal words. "If your heart is right," he declared, "if your thoughts are clean, the snake will not harm you. It will treat you as a friend. There is no question as to the truth of this. The snake knows what your intentions are. It knows that you are to be trusted. But if you have had evil thoughts and are not to be trusted, then you had better stay away. This is always true whenever a man has anything to do with an animal."

In conversation with another Hopi, an old friend, I learned that he had just trapped a fox. The pelt was now drying on a stretcher, and presently would be tanned by the captor. After that it would take its place as a part of a ceremonial costume, for which it was well adapted because it was neither too small, and therefore of little use, nor too large and thus likely to drag on the ground when attached to the back of a belt. The fox had been caught by one of its feet. My friend took it in his hands and carefully released it before burying its nose in the ground in order to bring about its death. "Didn't it try to bite you?" I asked. "Oh no! It was gentle and quiet. It was all right."

In the plant world, Hopi thought tends toward viewing various kinds of plants as groups, rather than as individual plants, toward corn as a crop rather than as a single plant, toward melons or beans as aggregates. This seems natural, since the individual animal readily gives an impression of specific personality, while the same is not likely to be true of a plant. There is less likelihood of ascribing a spirit form to the wild plants except in times when a certain species becomes economically significant in Hopi life. The wild flora is more likely to be viewed as an indefinite whole. Nevertheless, when a wild plant is cut off or dug up, as it is, for example, in securing a planting stick, tradition requires that it first be sprinkled with a bit of sacred meal, symbolizing a silent prayer to its spirit. It is a living thing, the work of the creator of all life, and is not to be wantonly destroyed.

When it comes to the celestial bodies and natural phenomena, the background handed down by Hopi custom and tradition is always present and exerts an unquestionable influence. The sun, the moon, the earth, certain stars—these have long since been given imaginative or spirit names, just as they have by many other peoples. As such, they enter into Hopi prayers and ceremonies, as well as mythology; but it would be a mistake to assume that there is no distinction between the object itself and that which its imaginative name signifies.

As a Hopi friend expresses it, "The sun, the moon, and the stars are the work of a great Power. This Power created them. We speak of the Mother Earth, but it is not the earth who created all the creatures that live on the earth. It is this same Power that

161

COYAWY'EMA

To most of his friends, he is Homer. Often his Hopi
name is shortened to Coyama, but its correct form is
the longer name given here. It is pronounced Coh-yah-
weye'-ee-mah, and means "Gray fox walking away."
He is a landscape painter, working in both oils and
water colors. In recent years he has been commissioned
to do murals in churches. His home is in Kiakochmovi.
In this portrait he is wearing the costume of the Hopi
band, in which he plays.

made the sun and moon and stars. That is what we worship—
the Great Power."

When, in a traditional marriage ceremony, a young man and
a young woman go at dawn to the edge of the mesa, to "pray to
the sun," they do not offer their prayers to the actual sun itself,
but to that which it signifies, to the warmth that it brings to the
earth, the plant and animal life that it makes possible, the opportunity for human existence and increase. This is the vital distinction, and this is what raises the Hopi attitude toward celestial
bodies above pagan worship. This also is an aspect which the
white observer may fail to understand.

Among the natural phenomena there are those which, by
their nature, can profoundly affect Hopi life and security. Rain
is one of these. In the midst of the difficulties that surround the
Hopi people, it is small wonder that prayers for rain should be
uttered. We ourselves, in similar circumstances, often follow the
same course. When calamity impends, we pray. When some one
whom we love is ill and threatened with death, we have recourse
to prayer, feeling in that act not only strength and encouragement
for ourselves but also increased hope for the one who is ill.

Among the Hopis some phenomena suggest by their character a likeness to some aspect of human life. Fleecy clouds, float-
ing high up in the sky, drifting across from the mountain peaks
toward Hopi homes, symbolize the spirits of human beings; and
so a cloud, *Omau'u* in Hopi language, becomes a spirit symbol,
worthy of prayers which themselves are of the spirit. A storm
cloud, which can bring life-saving rain, represents also the spirit
of rain, and to that spirit a message from the human spirit world
may rightly be addressed.

Hopi views as to the extent to which natural phenomena
can be influenced vary, I think, with the individual. With some

of the older men, whose formative years were spent in circumstances different in some ways from those now prevailing, views and beliefs encompass much. With younger men, the attitude, though one of belief, is less comprehensive. In any case, one important fact holds true for all Hopi people. While they consider that natural phenomena characteristically follow the laws of cause and effect, they also believe that on occasion, when there is sufficient reason and when circumstances are favorable, man can influence those phenomena. This may not happen often. It may require unusual conditions regarding both the reason for the desired outcome and the character of the invocation that man utters. But in Hopi beliefs, it can and does take place.

In the Hopi world the spirits identified with natural forces are for the most part benign. They are invoked for help and well-being, not propitiated out of terror and to avoid calamity. An exception is *Masau'u,* the spirit of fire, war, and death and the guardian of the underworld. Even here, it must be admitted, the province of this spirit includes that which, by nature, is foreign to happiness. As for the spirit which the Hopis call the Spider Grandmother, her realm is that of knowledge, of penetrating and shrewd understanding of all things both open and secret. If a man invokes her intercession, he must be prudent in his desires.

The spirit world as conceived of by the Hopis is free of the small demons which dog the lives of many Chinese—the imaginary evil beings who are forever threatening man, infesting the darkness, hiding in secret places, creeping up on him when he is not watching, slipping into his home, always ready to do him harm. The Hopi people do not feel called upon to pound on gongs in order to drive away pernicious demons.

Always, in Hopi belief, a man's thoughts have their effect

on his body and well-being. If they are happy and good, he will feel the benefit. If his thoughts are evil or unhappy, or even sad, he and his body will be harmed thereby. The sequence is one of cause and effect and is not to be abrogated or denied. The belief is not continually in a man's conscious thoughts; nevertheless, it is an ever-present background of conduct. It is not a formalized part of Hopi religion, for it is not set up as a specific creed. It simply stands as an accepted fact, which is everywhere recognized and which no doubt has been so accepted by untold generations. It is not an alien dogma transmitted to the Hopis by some other civilization within history.

In addition, the Hopis believe that through his thoughts a man can affect the life and bodily welfare of another person. If his thoughts and wishes toward that person are right and good, they will have beneficial effects, both on the one who wishes well and on the subject of his good thoughts. If they are evil, if he wishes harm to another, both he and the object of his destructive desires will suffer. The sequence is again one of cause and effect. The medium through which it operates is the spirit of the man who wishes ill and the spirit of the victim. The first suffers harm and of necessity transmits that harm to the second, and thus to the victim's body and well-being. Inevitably it follows that the man who harms another by this process pays an equal penalty himself, even while he is satisfying his desires. Of this fact he is bound to be aware.

It is just as possible for a man to wish ill to a group of people as it is to desire harm to an individual. In that case, the results are likely not to be so specific and destructive, perhaps because the power to do harm is too thinly spread. If, however, a group joins in wishing harm to a person or to another group, the consequences can be extensive and disastrous. Quarrels between two groups or factions, if they become bitter, can be destructive to both.

Sometimes in the past the misfortunes of a person or a family have been laid at the door of some individual who was believed to be responsible because of his evil thoughts. Seemingly this never reached the state of mass hysteria witnessed among our own people in the days of Salem witchcraft. But individual cases have occurred, and even today an example is not unheard of. Another similar situation sometimes results when a man threatens to bring sickness or disaster upon some person who is following a course which he is determined to block, and distressing fear can envelop the victim of the threats.

The penalty exacted from a man for his evil thoughts and deeds is paid by him here and now, rather than at some future time and place after his death. Part of that penalty lies in his own knowledge of his wrongdoing and his certain belief that he must pay the price. Part lies in the effect of his wrong desires upon his own life and well-being. Sickness or other misfortune will be his lot; his crops may fail or may be destroyed by storm or flood; accidents may befall him. There is no escaping the consequences; nor is there any agency, high or low, either in the spirit world or in the temporal, which can relieve him from his obligation. No one can give him absolution. A Hopi does not ask to be forgiven his sins; there is no such thing as forgiveness.

Sometimes the thought seems to appear that a man who has committed grave wrongs may, at his death, inhabit the body of an animal, such as the coyote, which is viewed as a treacherous or unworthy creature; but generally the concept of transmigration is not widely held. When a man dies, he ceases to inhabit his body, which therefore no longer has any significance. If he is an old man, he has completed his present mission and is passing on to further activity elsewhere. This is not sad or deplorable but may even be to him a welcome change. If death comes to a child, especially to a young child, the feeling is one of regret because the child was not able to complete its life. In such case, the spirit of the child may remain in or around the home for a time, just as if it still inhabited the discarded body. There is no belief that the spirit of one who dies enters, at that moment, the body of a newly-born baby. Reincarnation, in that sense, is not a part of Hopi belief.

Immortality, however, is firmly and universally accepted. In fact, there is no real dividing line between life now and life later. They are one and the same thing. That which exists here and which can be experienced through our physical senses is only one aspect of existence. The spirit aspect is just as real even though you cannot see it. If the body ceases to function, the spirit is not changed thereby. As some one has said, the Hopi view may be likened to the thought that, when a man dies, he merely wakes up.

Since the spirit is such an important part of human life, and since its existence is not contingent upon that of the body, it follows that on occasion the spirit may leave the body for a time and later return to it. This concept is accepted among many or perhaps most Hopis. To a smaller extent the temporary departure may be evidenced by dreams. Usually such a dream is concerned only with the individual himself and does not involve matters of consequence to others. In a larger way, a spirit journey without the body may occur at an individual's time of critical illness, when he is on the borderline of life and death. Such an experience is rare or, at least, is rarely reported. Even in this case, the subject matter of the experience is likely to concern only the individual and his future. Apparently there is no account of a great

disclosure affecting all the Hopi people, such as the historic revelations upon which some religions of Europe and Asia are based.

In all matters relating to the spirit world prayer plays a
significant part, but it must be remembered that, as the Hopi
thinks of it, prayer is more than the inattentive reciting of words
or phrases. To pray is to desire, and at the same time to will,
completely and unequivocally; the three are synonymous. Prayer
without desire is a contradiction, and prayer without will is
empty. There is no middle ground.

Mass prayer is at the root of the major Hopi ceremonies. It is directed toward the various objectives which are
essential or desirable in Hopi life—security, abundant crops,
health, long life, and children. It emphasizes increase of needed
plants, useful animals, and human beings, and seeks to strengthen
the natural forces which can bring about these ends. In addition
it seeks the well-being of all human creatures everywhere.

Through simultaneous participation by many persons, the
prayer is given added strength. In fact, this aspect is so important in the Hopi view that any deviation from it, whether
willful or inadvertent, is serious and is bound to impair effective-
ness. Where many people pray together, each man must have a
clear conscience, and he must not have any sad or evil thoughts. In
Hopi practice it is permissible for one person attending a ceremony to ask another, "Have your thoughts been right and
good?" Not only is the question allowable and not uncommon,
but the one who is questioned must and will withdraw if the
answer cannot honestly be in the affirmative. "In this way," say
the Hopis, "prayer will be able to win a response." The matter
is recognized by everyone as being too important to be denied.

The obligation to maintain correct thoughts and desires applies with special emphasis to the leader of a ceremony. In essence,

he is the representative of the entire group. That is one of the reasons why he is recognized as a leader. His prayers are uttered for all in the group, and must have a quality commensurate with his status and authority. Both he and all others who enact specific roles in a ceremony must follow definite rules in their activities before the rites take place. Those who merely are present in order to look on must be attentive and must participate in spirit. Anything less than this works harm. In this belief lies the feeling of many Hopis, that the presence of unsympathetic whites, though permitted, is unfortunate.

In this connection there are thoughtful Hopis who feel that a householder who accepts money from a white for a seat on his roof at a ceremony violates Hopi traditions. There are many who consider it wrong to sell any merchandise near the plaza where a ceremony is taking place. I was surprised one time to hear the comments of a group of young men who were standing in the outskirts of a village, in whose plaza a ceremony was in progress. They were eighteen or twenty years old and might have been thought of as less conservative and exacting in their views. An older man had set up a stand near by and was selling soft drinks. "He should not do that," declared one of the young men. "It's wrong to do that when a dance is taking place." The others joined him in his comments. All of them were earnest in their disapproval.

A multitude of details clothe the major ceremonies, both the part which is given in the plaza and is open to the public and, no doubt, the much longer part which is enacted in the kivas and is not public. The acts performed by the participants, the details of costume, the accessories, the prerogatives and duties of individuals taking part—all these are fixed by tradition. Each has a meaning and significance in one way or another. Together

HO'TEWA

To the White friend, he is "Ralph"; to the Hopis, especially the older men, he is Ho'tewa, which is pronounced Hoh'-tee-wah and which means "Arrow finished." His travels have taken him to many places in the Southwest and have made him well informed in both White and Indian ways. Unmarried, he is sixty-five years old. His home is at the foot of Third Mesa, in New Oraibi, properly called Kiakochmovi.

they form a ritual which is the essence of Hopi religion, in drama form, just as the rituals of other religions throughout the world symbolize the sacred history of a religion and the beliefs and prayers of its adherents. That we of the white race do not understand the details of a Hopi ceremony should not mean that we doubt its authenticity or its significance.

During a part of the year the masked figures called Kachinas appear in ceremonies. They vary widely in their importance. Basically, those which are most significant represent beings from the spirit world, sometimes the spirits of those who have gone on from their physical existence, sometimes others which are not so identified. Always, however, they have a role to play as guardians, protectors, and teachers of human beings now on earth. They represent the wisdom and strength of an invisible world, which is greater and more informed than its visible counterpart.

It seems that a man who participates in a ceremony feels that he is uplifted out of himself while he is taking part. If he enacts a certain character, he is, for a time, that personage. If, as such, he would possess powers denied him otherwise, he genuinely feels that those powers during that period become a part of his endowment. Shortly after the Snake Ceremony in one of the villages, I was talking with the man who was leader of the Snake priests. "You know," he said, "as soon as I entered the plaza I felt as if my body was transformed. I felt as if my feet did not touch the earth. Everything was different. I could do things that I could not ordinarily do." As a matter of fact, I saw him in that ceremony pick up a rattler which seemed bent on mischief, stroke its body once or twice, and hand it, quiet and limp, to another participant. That this ceremony can reasonably be considered a religious rite may be difficult of acceptance, but it must be remembered that the snakes are conceived of as messengers entrusted with prayers.

The Hopis

Although these elaborate rites are so firmly entrenched in Hopi religion and although they require long training on the part of those who enact major roles, the Hopis have never witnessed the rise of a special class of priests who are set apart from other men as divine beings, comparable to the Buddhist priests of Tibet and other Oriental countries. In daily life, their ceremonial leaders are no different from other men in their ordinary activities and obligations. They may command respect beyond the ordinary, but this is because of their character and attainments, rather than because of their office. Attainments bring about recognition and position; the reverse, in which position confers recognition, is not the sequence.

There is nothing to indicate that a commanding spiritual leader, a Messiah, has ever arisen among the Hopi people. If such an event did take place at some period in the past there would not, of course, be any written records, but presumably other evidence would exist. There is a tradition that a great leader would some day appear who would conduct the Hopis to a place or a life in which worldly troubles would come to an end. Sometimes this anticipated Messiah is conceived of as a man of the white race. But whether this concept actually dates back to prehistoric times is a question that cannot be answered with certainty.

A woman whom I chanced to meet, an associate of a national organization which is concerned with promoting religious education, asked me about the religious training of Hopi young folk. "Do they have something like our Sunday school?" she inquired. The answer is No. The Hopis do not set apart a Sabbath day which is devoted to spiritual matters. Every day has its worldly interests, and along with them, welded with them and a part of them, are the aspects which relate to the spirit world. The two are not separable. A Hopi boy and girl receive their instruction from early childhood, first in the home and, later for the boy, in the kiva. It is all a unified training toward a happy and useful life, with no formal distinction between practical affairs and those of the spirit because the two are indissolubly related. The objective is to learn how to follow "the Hopi way."

What then is the traditional Hopi way? Its aims are a course of conduct which will lead to well-being and happiness, a course that has been set forth in other religions which are very old and which have crystallized their teachings in the written word. It has a certain parallel, for example, in the Road to Nirvana as conceived by Gautama, more than two thousand years ago—right speech, conduct, aims, effort, and state of mind. It coincides with many of our own Ten Commandments.

To the Hopis the essence of it all is to seek what they term "a good heart," a way of life in which a man is honest, truthful, considerate, gentle with children, understanding with those who are old, free from sadness, fear, or harmful thoughts, constantly aware that he is a part of a great, immortal spirit world.

MISSIONARY

"How many of the Hopis are Christians?"—this question is often asked, perhaps doubtfully, because the questioner is thinking of ceremonies which he has heard about, and which he looks upon as pagan rites, perhaps hopefully, since this is the twentieth century and we have been neighbors to these people for more than a hundred years.

The answer is not easily arrived at with certainty. A Hopi may attend a service in a mission chapel of one of the familiar denominations. He may join in the singing and listen attentively to what the missionary has to say. He may be friendly and, within limits, receptive or even responsive. Yet he may not have accepted the faith, especially if, as may be true, it demands that he abandon the beliefs in which he was raised, the concept of an all-embracing spirit world in which all creatures and all natural forces participate.

The total number of Hopis is about four thousand, five hundred. It is reasonably certain that the number of actual Christian converts among the Hopis is as many as forty-five, but not as many as ninety—between one and two per cent—which is not an impressive percentage.

Missionary

In this connection it must be remembered that the status in the pueblos of New Mexico is completely different from that in the Hopi villages. When the Spanish came back to New Mexico after the uprising of 1680, their padres incorporated the pueblo population into the Catholic church. They built or rebuilt missions, gave the people Spanish names, and made communicants of them. This situation still prevails. The pueblo inhabitants attend Catholic services, although they also maintain and attend as many of their own original ceremonies as have survived. But the Spaniards and their padres did not cross over and occupy the Hopi country, although the Hopis fully expected them and established villages on top of the mesas for defense. Spanish names did not develop. The Catholic church occupies a position today among the Hopis which is no different from that of Protestant denominations who maintain missions.

Since the various denominations of the Christian religion have long since crystallized into divergent details of practice and creed, it follows that the missions now present, representing several of those denominations, reflect specific and different dogmas.

The missionaries themselves must be at least equally divergent in their methods and attitudes, since each must reflect his own individual background and personality. If the man was born a zealot he is not likely to become anything less when working with an alien people. If he was brought up in tolerance he may grow in sympathy and understanding, in spite of the fact that he speaks for a specific creed. It is not possible to generalize about the missionaries, nor would it be reasonable to attempt to analyze specific missions, since no one can know all of the factors operating in the endeavors of each one, or all of the detailed results of each one's activities. With one exception, denominations will not be referred to by name in this chapter.

The Hopis

The exception arises from a conversation I had with two young missionaries of the Mormon Church. It is related not because of any predilection toward the Mormon faith or any special admiration for its tenets, but because it is illuminating. The young men were stationed at that time in one of the Hopi villages, and I ran across them in the village store. Our conversation turned to churches, creeds, and Hopi ceremonies.

"Tell me," I said, "do you consider that the Hopi is on his way to eternal punishment unless he accepts your faith?"

"Oh no," they said, "we do not believe in the idea that a man is bound for either Heaven or Hell."

"Do you consider," I continued, "that the Hopis have no religion; that their beliefs are pagan?"

"On the contrary," they declared, "the Hopi religion is a good deal like the Mormon faith. It does not include some things in which we believe. The stages in the road to Paradise, for example. But much of it is in agreement with our own. We do not have any quarrel with the Hopi beliefs."

Later, when there was access to a library, I looked up the Mormon religion and found these passages among others in a statement of that church's articles of faith:

"We believe in . . . prophesy, revelation, visions, healing . . .

"We claim the privilege of worshiping . . . according to the dictates of our own conscience, and allow all men the same privilege, let them worship how, when, or what they may.

"We believe in . . . doing good to all men."

I do not know how consistently or completely these pronouncements are lived up to. The Mormon church has its details of required procedure for its members, and its missionaries must be constantly aware of these; they must believe them to be important to proposed converts, as well as to themselves. But the tolerance expressed in the quoted articles of the Mormon faith is akin to Hopi views.

Inevitably the missions in an Indian country are likely to represent narrow as well as broad views. This has been true among the Hopis. No doubt a missionary with narrow and rigid views, trained to consider his faith the only one that is allowable, finds it difficult to look upon Hopi beliefs with tolerance. Literally, he is unable to understand, and his mind is closed to any sympathetic interpretation of what he sees and hears. This rigidity of view, when combined with the driving fervor of a zealot, leads at times to acts which, to the white observer, seem unfortunate, even though the Hopis themselves may not show resentment. Through intolerance, the cause of the missionary would seem to be defeating itself. Incidents such as the following, although infrequent, stand out because of their harshness.

A ceremony which is significant in Hopi thoughts was taking place one day in a village on one of the mesas. In the ritual, as is true with other Hopi ceremonies, the importance of fertility was stressed, the significance of increase for all life, plant and animal, from corn to butterfly to human beings. A missionary group with a portable organ took up a position adjacent to the ceremony and tried to drown out the chants of the participants in the ritual.

Once a little Hopi girl of grade school age was killed by the overturning of a truck. Along with other children, she was on her way to see a desert rodeo. The day happened to be Sunday, which is not considered a day apart by the Hopis. A missionary preached for an hour in the presence of the bereaved family, saying that, if the child had been where she should have been, in Sunday school, she would still have been alive.

Sometimes it appears that one missionary is more interested

POLIES'TEWA

His home is on the elevated plateau of Third Mesa, in the ancient village of Old Oraibi. The house that he and his wife occupy has been standing for many generations. The storage room attached to it is exceptionally large and, in season, is well stocked with the products of his fields. It is likely to hold, also, a sample of his expert weaving. His name is pronounced Poh-lee-es'-tee-wah and means "Butterfly that has settled down." His age is about eighty-five.

in thwarting another than in any other endeavor of the moment. A young missionary who came out second best in such a contest was telling me about it. He had been working a long time, he said, to convert a prominent Hopi. Finally the man had given his promise to embrace the faith. It happened that the man's wife was about to have a baby. The other missionary, older and more experienced in strategy, took advantage of the situation. He said to the Hopi, "You have promised that young fellow that you will join his church. Your wife is going to have a baby. Unless you renounce your promise either your wife or the baby will die." The Hopi hesitated, and meanwhile the baby was born. A few days later it became ill and died. The older missionary lost no time in reminding the husband of the warning that he had received and the penalty for not heeding that warning. "Now," the younger missionary complained, "I'll never get that man to join. There's no use working on him any more."

Unquestionably these incidents represent only one part of mission activity among the Hopis—an aspect which is not necessarily representative. Another part would show more tolerance, more appreciation of the inner meaning of Hopi rituals, more realization of the significance of Hopi concepts, and more understanding of Hopi beliefs. This other part is also less likely to be emphasized in the mind of the white observer because it is painted in quiet tones.

Many thoughtful Hopis, especially those of middle age or younger, seem to have an open mind toward the broad foundations of Christian belief. In a quiet way, they have listened and considered. They do not find antagonism between their own traditional concept of a great Power and the fundamentals of Christian religion.

I have listened to the observations of a Hopi friend who is in his sixties. His own small children have been baptized in the Catholic faith. He does not in the least object to this. It will do them no harm. As for himself his mind is open. He looks out upon the world and the universe as the manifestation of a Power which has always been the object of his prayers. He may in time accept the specific faith of a Christian church, but meanwhile he is content to wait and reflect.

That the missionaries are not easily discouraged is abundantly evident. One of the missions, for example, has been laboring since before the beginning of this century. It works aggressively and has an active affiliation with its parent denomination. It has a sizable church building. Its congregation numbers about twenty-five persons.

"Are they all members of the church?" I asked.

"Well, a good many of them are—but they are still Hopis!"

Apparently this mission has averaged about one actual convert in two years. They consider that the adult Hopi is pretty difficult to win over and that the undertaking ought to start with the children, who presumably would be more pliable. They drew up plans to meet this situation by starting a small grade school.

In general the reaction of the Hopi people to the missions in the reservation seems, outwardly at least, to be one of friendly tolerance. The missionary has his own way of existence and, like any other human being, is entitled to follow his own devices. No one should tell him what he ought or ought not to do. If he fails to understand Hopi beliefs, that is his misfortune but also his privilege. If he infringes on sacred Hopi rituals, he is harming himself, not the ritual which is too strong to suffer much harm in that way. If a Hopi chooses to join a mission, that is his privilege. No one will think less or more of him because of his decision.

All of this can of course be judged only from outward reactions. The matter is not likely to be discussed with the white visitor, even the white friend of long standing. Indeed, such a friend will not bring it up and ask questions because he knows that he would get nowhere and would lose standing in so doing. I suspect that the subject is seldom brought up by a Hopi in talking with his own people.

If a Hopi has adopted the religion taught by a missionary, you may have evidence of that fact only through his attendance at mission services. In other ways he may seem no different from his neighbors. He may indeed continue his interest in the ancient ceremonies, not as an active participant, but as an appreciative spectator. At the same time, he may be a devout and consistent communicant of his mission.

A Hopi may become an assistant at a mission, or he may take it over during the missionary's prolonged absence. If so, there seems to be no marked reaction on the part of his neighbors. A Hopi may break away from a mission to which he has been attached and start one of his own. Again there may be no open comment. Whether other Hopis feel that he has done an injustice to Hopi beliefs can be no more than surmised. Singularly, the white, who should be a disinterested observer, may be the one who shrugs his shoulders as if, in his way of thinking, the Hopi who abandons his traditional beliefs has moved down the scale a step or two. Unfortunately, we of the white race are not as tolerant as our Indian friends.

As to the intangible effects of missionary activity on Hopi ways and character and the tendencies which they may help to stimulate or suppress, full appraisal is not possible. The best that can be done is to estimate from observations or fragmentary evidence, which may lead one in any direction he would like to go, depending on preconceived ideas or natural inclination.

The Hopis

Every time that I have opportunity I visit a certain Hopi man and his wife. It would be difficult to find a gentler, more understanding, or more rewarding couple. They attend a mission, the head of which is anything but broad or understanding. Evidently the influence of the missionary, whatever else it may be, has not been visibly harmful to these people.

What then is the effect brought about by the impact of missionary activity on Hopi life? Unquestionably an appreciable part of it, a part which may often be too unobtrusive to attract much attention, is constructive and good. Another part, which sometimes is in evidence, is unfortunate and can be damaging. Up to the present moment, the Hopi people as a whole, especially the older generations, seem not to be widely affected either way.

Meanwhile, the Hopi concepts continue to find embodiment in a cycle of ceremonies which express, in dramatic form, the ancient Hopi beliefs and which afford appealing experiences to the mesa-dwellers.

IMPACT

IN THEIR OWN WAY the Hopis have a well-developed civilization.

Many persons will take exception to this statement, especially those who judge from a distance or who see only the surface—the small houses, the lack of bathrooms, telephones or electricity, the dependence on slow means of transportation, the continued adherence to elaborate ceremonies. If you use as your standard the advances achieved by the Western world in science, invention, and the mechanics of living, you will feel that the Hopis have not made much progress in civilization, but if you will lay aside material standards for the moment and base your appraisal on that which is largely intangible, which is not arresting in a visible way, you may conclude that these people have evolved and maintain a way of life which is worthy of a considerable measure of admiration.

It is illuminating to compare the white man's way and the Hopi's in the various aspects of human existence, to observe the impact of the former on the latter, and to discover what the Hopi manner of thought may offer that is sound and logical and should be preserved for others to consider.

The Hopis

As we all know, the mainspring of our Western civilization is change. Always that which is different and better must be sought and found. This is the foundation on which our tremendous advances have been built. Within a few decades it has given us the prevention of many serious human diseases, prolonging human life. It has given new speed to transportation, both on the surface of the earth and in the air. It has built multi-lane highways, has harnessed rivers for thirsty land, and has made it possible for human vision to span the continent. In a thousand ways it has made human life easier and more secure. To all this we point with honest and justifiable pride, declaring that this is the surpassing achievement of the white race, as indeed it is.

Hopi civilization, on the other hand, is completely opposite. It maintains no laboratories for chemical research, invents no complicated machines, takes out no patents. Hopi thoughts and abilities do not run in that direction. Rather, they are concerned, continually and profoundly, with living successfully in the world as it is. They seek to work in harmony with the natural forces, great and small, not to harness them or to change them. They look for their guidance to the experiences and achievements of their own people down through the centuries. Their most cherished objective is a useful, well-poised, and happy life, which has in it no element of worry or fear and which is a harmonious part of an ever-present and all-pervading spirit world.

Inevitably our white civilization derives much of its impetus and progress from competition. This is its principal source of energy, and this prevails in science as well as in business and manufacture. The man who is to make his mark must excel in his initiative and in the productive utilization of his talents. He must get ahead, which means of course that he must also get ahead of the other fellow.

Impact

In the Hopi way of thinking this idea has little appeal, and its results, as he views them, have poor standing. He notes that sometimes the white man, in driving to get ahead, is less than honest, that often he is far less than considerate. Since unquestionably this has been true at times in Hopi contacts with the whites, it is always to be reckoned with. This characteristic of the whites, in the Hopi view, harms human relations, and thus a continuing price must be paid. So sure is the Hopi of this weakness in the white race that one must be a very good friend indeed to be accorded such complete confidence as never to be subject to any cloud of question. The fact that, in the white world, competition is responsible for great material advances does not count heavily with the Hopis. It may be admitted, but he questions whether the advances are overwhelmingly important. At what price have they been achieved? As a Hopi friend said one time, speaking of motor cars, airplanes, conflicts and wars, "What is it, anyhow, that everybody wants?"

The idea of competitive awards, of medals and prizes and names on a scroll, finds little or no approval among the Hopis. They disbelieve in it as much for adults in their crafts or other activities as for children in school. The reason lies in the belief that those who fail to win will feel inferior, which is harmful to them. If they feel envious toward the one who wins, not only will that do them harm, but at the same time will injure the winner. If a man raises a superior field of corn he may rightly take pride in it, but he will do wrong if he compares it with his neighbor's, even in his own mind. The achievement itself is the only allowable reward.

This belief is manifestly at the opposite pole from that of our race. Not only do we encourage and believe in competition, but in large industries we require it. Justly, we consider that it

KIASHO'INEM

Her name is pronounced Kee-ash-hoh'-ĭ-nem and means "Parrot ready to fly." Using her husband's name, as most Hopi women now prefer, she is Edith Duw-yenie, a capable young matron who has adopted White ways but has not forgotten Hopi customs. Her home is in Hotevilla.

has erected the vast and elaborate house in which we live. It should be noted that the Hopi view does not substitute a regulated economy. It looks wholly to the individual. He and he alone determines his course, just as he alone reaps the consequences, whether good or bad.

It follows that any organized manufacturing remotely resembling that to which we are accustomed has no place in Hopi life or thoughts. In a small way, it was tried once and failed. While many years have passed since that event, the underlying tendencies have not changed. I doubt if any Hopi whom I have ever met would care for the routine of a production line. Probably he would be reliable and painstaking, but his heart would not be in it. The Hopi men are not potential factory employees—not those of the present generations at any rate.

Typically, Hopi men are self-employed. Typically also, a man does not have others working for him. The Hopi spirit of independent effort and reward is too thoroughly ingrained to make that relationship natural. A Hopi man will work on the road with his truck. He may take a job in town, as a carpenter or house-painter, for example, because he needs cash in order to take care of his family, in the face of restricted flocks brought about by government regulations, or because he must support an increased number of dependents following the death of a breadwinner. He will be an industrious worker, since industry is a part of his heritage, but, if he can, he will return to his former independent way of life. I know a man who spent three or four years as an occasional character actor in Hollywood movie productions. He is now back in his own village, raising his crops, hauling water from a spring, herding his sheep, and feeding the captive eagles on his housetop.

Our white race, also, has its self-employed, its farmers and merchants, doctors and lawyers, but many or most of these employ others, which the Hopis almost never do. The words "self-employed" have a different meaning for the two peoples. As for the rest of our race, they work for wages or for salaries. They are the clerks, the teachers, the ministers, and the great body of industrial workers. Neither in the nature of their work relationships nor in the trend of their thoughts do they parallel the Hopis. They are part of a vast and complicated organization, and they must think in those terms. They may or may not belong to the CIO or the AF of L, but they are units in an intricate operating machine. The Hopi is both employer and employee, producer and consumer, manufacturer and market.

As soon as the white man made contact with the Hopis he began to institute change. This was his obligation and his mission. He is still planning, proposing, or enacting change, and the Hopi is still reluctantly agreeing to, fearing, or sometimes resisting those changes. If he agrees to them, he is likely to do so with the feeling that the matter is inevitable and he might as well make the best of it. If he resists he is compelled by no passing whim of the moment but by convictions which may be as firmly fixed as the bedrock of a mountain.

The tenacity with which a Hopi holds to his convictions is well known to all white persons who have had any experience with these people. The man may take a long time to make a decision while he considers the circumstances and weighs the evidence, or he may come to a quick decision, if the matter lies in a field wherein he already has strong beliefs. But once he has decided, he is likely to remain adamant from that time on. Even if he has arrived at his conclusion on a mistaken premise, you will find it difficult or often impossible to correct that premise.

I had ample evidence of that characteristic in a personal experience one time. A Hopi family had become delightful and valued friends of mine. I was invariably welcomed in my visits at their home. Then something that I did was misinterpreted. To my surprise and regret, the next time I called the door was opened only a few inches and promptly closed. When I asked for the reason, I was told what I had done. When I insisted that I had done no such thing I got nowhere. When other Hopis tried to intervene in my behalf they also got nowhere. The subject was closed, apparently for all time, and remains closed to this day.

When a Hopi believes that another Hopi has done him an injustice, he never forgets the incident or cancels the debt of injury; it stands and cannot be changed. Unlike a debt of money or goods, it cannot be paid up and forgotten. In the long contact with the white race, this inflexibility has created difficulties and erected barriers which seemingly must await the coming of other generations for correction. I listened one day to an elderly Hopi friend relate an incident of his youth in which a white authority had neglected, as he believed, to pay him for a service rendered. What the merits were I do not know, but the fact remained that after fifty years my friend still carried the incident in his mind, undiminished.

If an individual Hopi will cling to an idea, right or wrong, which is based on a personal incident, it can be taken for granted that in major matters a group will be no less tenacious in its convictions. Sometimes this has been embarrassingly true in the relationship of one or another part of the Hopi population to white authority.

Naturally the whites who are in official contact with the Hopis seek to bring about improvements in the reservation, improvements which the white man looks upon as essential. But in the Hopi view, a change is always to be examined critically and always, in some aspects, is hazardous. You may succeed in learning precisely what it involves now, but you cannot know what it may lead to in the future. Eventually it may turn out to be something that is not at all desirable, and, by that time, you can no longer do anything about it.

A section of road provides an illustration—a part of the road which connects the Agency, at Keams Canyon, with the various Hopi villages. Originally, it was just a desert road, largely made by scraping up adjacent soil. Gradually it was improved in some stretches by the building of culverts and the hauling on of suitable material. Later, more serious work was undertaken and was put through where the road made a long climb and descent, crossing two mesas. Although tricky in certain parts after a rain, the highway then served the needs of Agency employees fairly well and provided, for the Hopis, easy access from one village to another, which they utilized fully, since they like to visit their friends and relatives and to attend the various ceremonies.

Recently there came to the area an ambitious project for road construction, involving new and elaborate highway relocating and building over the two mesas, and calling for skillful engineering if the road were to qualify eventually as an up-to-date through highway. Since the road connects on the east with Gallup and on the west with a much-traveled route to Grand Canyon, the idea of a fast thoroughfare from the east to the Canyon may not have been unthought of.

All of this, so far as the Hopis were concerned, went along without too much reaction, up to a certain point. That point was the route which the engineers selected for the climb up Second Mesa from the east. The difficulty lay in the fact that the highway would cut through the site where the village now on top of the mesa once stood. "This," said the Hopi men, "we cannot permit.

Impact

Scores of houses which our ancestors built occupy that site. That is the home place of our village. It must not be desecrated. The engineers must find a different route. We would prefer not to see the highway built at all. It will only bring fast automobile traffic and will do our people no good. We will not say that it shall not be built. But we do say that it must not destroy the village from which our people came."

There was no modifying this conviction or altering the requirement that had been laid down. Apparently the only thing to do was to set the engineers at work again.

Water for the mesa villages affords another provocative problem. Nine of the Hopi villages are perched on the elevated tops of three mesas, several hundred feet above the adjacent country. Springs which have been used since prehistoric times are situated part way down or at the foot of the precipitous escarpments. In one of the nine villages there is a hand pump which draws its water from a spring a little way down the slope. For the remainder, trails or roads lead to the springs. They get their water by way of their own legs or by those of a burro, or, if a truck is available they haul it that way. Observing this, the white visitor is certain to exclaim, "Why doesn't the government drill a well and install a power pump? They are spending money on other improvements such as roads, why not on water supply?"

The Indian Service has given the matter serious study. The geologists and engineers know pretty well what strata carry water. The rock formations which would have to be tapped lie at a considerable depth, perhaps two thousand feet or more, since this is desert country, but that fact is no insurmountable barrier. At the Hopi high school water is pumped from a similar depth. But in these villages a different factor enters. The people look upon their springs as the very life-blood of their existence. Because of the vital part that springs have played since earliest times, they occupy a position which is sacred.

"What will happen if you drill a well?" they say. "Suppose it dries up our springs. You state that this would not make any difference because the well would take the place of the springs, and a power pump would provide plenty of water. But suppose the pump fails. When it wears out who will provide a new one? Suppose the water in the well gives out, and we have neither springs nor well. Suppose that the water from the well is not good water. Suppose it is full of salt like the well that the white man dug on the road to the Grand Canyon. Then we would have no water at all, and our villages would have to be abandoned. How can you guarantee that nothing like this would ever happen? Why should we agree to something that may destroy our homes and our lives? It is not bad for our people to carry water from a spring. It is good for the children to know about water and to learn not to waste it. They get good exercise from going to the spring. Our older folks, too, forget their years because they still can help to bring water."

After all, the white man, though well aware of the benefits that abundant water can provide, and convinced that it is essential in modern living, may nevertheless find food for thought in some of the Hopi contentions. In any event, no wells have yet been drilled.

For many years the Hopi people were not accorded the right to vote, although they were required to meet the obligations of citizenship. Congress, through an enabling act, said that they were qualified and therefore must assume the duties of citizenship, but ratification by the state, which would give them also the rights as well as the obligations, did not come for twenty-five years. When it did come, it was viewed by the Hopis as something long overdue, rather than something new. They had done their part, but the other fellow had taken a quarter of a century to do his.

Nevertheless, active citizenship, in the view of a number of Hopis, involves various matters which are open to question. It is all right to control your own destiny, if you can, but when somebody makes you a present, you are pretty certain to find that there are strings attached. These may not be evident at the moment, but some time or other they will show up. To the Hopis, there is no gift that has no element of obligation. A gift is always an exchange of some kind or other.

One aspect of citizenship, a vital part as we think of it, is the white man's concept of majority rule. This concept runs counter to ancient Hopi beliefs, wherein a man is entitled not only to make his own decisions but to follow his own course of conduct based on those decisions. There are many Hopis who realize fully that, by some means, unified action ought to be obtained. They recognize, in principle, the value of personal independence, but they feel that you cannot in that way solve some of the problems that today lie before the entire Hopi tribe. There are other Hopis who are deeply convinced that a person must retain sovereignty, that only in this way can the wisdom of older men be made effective, and that majority rule may represent only numbers, not experience and judgment. Belief among the Hopis today is divided.

Many Hopis are convinced that action by a majority is the way to modify regulations which they believe to be unwise, to prevent other requirements which might be proposed in the future, and to bring about necessary group action, as in the case of land claims. Many consider that they have been obliged to accept rules and orders which they might have averted. With earnest conviction, they point to the assumed boundaries of the Hopi

PAYES'TEWA

His name is pronounced Pah-yes'-tee-wah, and it means "Water that is standing on the ground." Often he is known by his childhood name, Poli, which means "Butterfly." He is widely known, not only in the Hopi country, but in some of the pueblos of New Mexico. Speaking English fluently, he was a member of the first class of the first government school established in the Hopi reservation. He is a grandson of the famous leader, Tuba. His age is eighty-seven. His home is in Moenkopi.

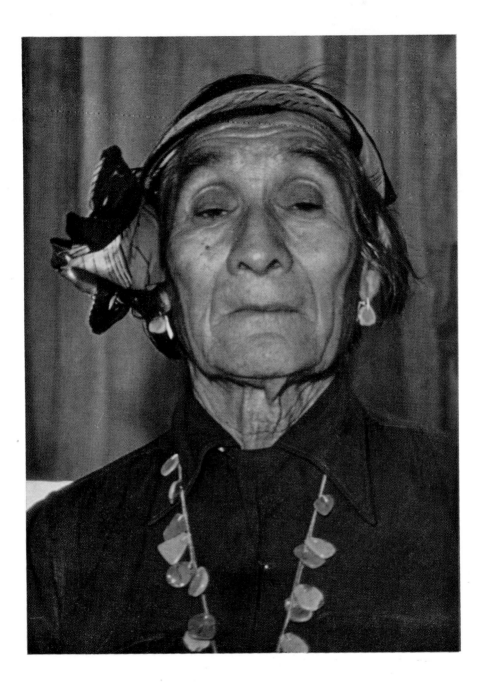

reservation as defined by an executive order in 1888. "Our region was not just that small area," they say. "For centuries we occupied an area many times that size. Our prehistoric villages prove this. If our people had been organized they could have prevented this wrong. Later we were ordered to cut down our flocks, and to destroy many of our sheep and horses. We should have been able to do something about that order."

The workings of democratic procedure among the Hopis present an anomaly. In our white world we look upon political campaigns as not only natural, but desirable. To a Hopi, the notion that a man may or should campaign for himself is completely foreign. The office seeks the man, not the man the office. There may be earnest and prolonged discussion and argument about the solution of a problem, and such discussion may be intense or even bitter, but this is different from a man's setting himself up to conduct an organized campaign for votes in competition with a rival. Something approaching this has developed recently, as the plan of an elected council has been under trial. Nevertheless, it is not the traditional Hopi procedure.

Even in the matter of a man's name the ancient Hopi way is different from ours. We maintain family names, carried on through successive generations. The custom lends itself to democratic workings, to the keeping of essential records. A wife takes a man's name when she marries him, the children are known by the same name, and thus our records are kept straight. A Hopi is given his adult name at a traditional ceremony. It has nothing to do with the name of his father or that of his mother. In recent years, though the old custom is not discarded, white names have been superimposed and wives have often taken their husbands' names. Sometimes, also, a son is now taking the father's name and adding the word "junior" or not bothering to make any distinction. Presumably, democracy is furthered and bookkeeping in in the Indian Service is facilitated, but one may regret the submergence of the old descriptive custom.

Some other effects of intercourse with white men are more far-reaching. The lure of substantial funds from the sale or lease of natural resources is one of these. For a period of years experts from various oil companies spent many weeks or months each year studying the reservation for oil indications. Through several summers they made their headquarters at the place where I was staying. Groups or individuals explored separately, theoretically in secret, one from another. Eventually one of them told me that all of them had decided on three or four areas where they were convinced that oil domes existed, far below the surface of the ground. It was understood that some companies stood ready to pay a rather large cash bonus, in addition to royalty, if the Hopis would unite and agree to a contract, under supervision of the Indian Service, and if their relationship with the Navajos living in the area were straightened out.

But would the Hopis unite? There was reason to doubt that they would. Conscientiously a number of Hopis feared what would happen, especially to their young folk. They could point to the consequences of oil leases and easy money in the case of other Indians. If the money were held in trust and used wisely for the welfare of the Hopis as a group, perhaps it would be all right, but how could they be sure that this would be done, then or in the future? There would always be pressure to relax the restrictions. People would take sides, and after a while there would be hard feelings and conflicts, which would cause harm to both sides. The availability of a lot of money would be a strong temptation. If money were ever divided among individuals, no doubt it would help some who would make good use of it, but it would ruin others.

A similar potential situation lay in the possibility that a large sum of money might be obtained from a settlement with the federal government for land taken from the Hopis. Some were eager to see a settlement secured, believing that the money could be managed to achieve lasting benefits. Others were firm in the conviction that irreparable harm would result.

While I was visiting in the reservation, a Hopi delegation made a trip to Salt Lake City to appear before a federal judge to secure authorization that would empower them to make a contract with a legal firm for presentation of land claims. The members of the delegation were earnest and sincere men. They represented seven of the twelve Hopi villages. "We are sure," they said, "that much can be done for our people. This is our chance to get those things done." The other five villages decided not to take part in the move, and these also were represented by equally earnest and sincere men, who believed that the money, if obtained, would lead to harm. "We cannot be sure," they said, "what will happen in the future. Our people have always taken care of themselves without dependence on others. If this money is made available we will find ourselves obligated to do things that will not be good for us."

In a personal and more subtle fashion, Hopi ways have been further influenced by white developments. It is not difficult to determine that a very old Hopi is old enough to be entitled to a monthly pension. It may be quite true that he is no longer able to support himself fully, and that he needs certain help. His grandchildren or other relatives, who would be expected to provide the necessary help under the old Hopi custom, may readily feel that a check from the government might as well be accepted since it seems to be obtainable and customary with other people. When the checks begin to arrive, they may, however, make little if any difference in the life of the old Hopi. He continues to work to the extent that he is able. The only result seems to be the breakdown of the traditional sense of responsibility on the part of his grandchildren or other relatives.

The effect of this on the traditional Hopi standards seems to be insidious and serious. To begin with, the Hopis are thrifty people. Because of their environment, they have had to be thrifty; they have had to make the most of their resources, to get the most out of their fields and crops, to barter successfully, and to secure the maximum out of any trade. This is the foundation of their economic success. Therefore, when a government check is offered, it has the aspect of a successful trade. Here is something that can be had for nothing. Increasingly, it seems, even some of the older Hopis feel a subtle demoralizing influence from this. With some, it tends to reduce initiative, especially in carrying on the crafts which for so long have been the major source of cash income. This bad effect is not yet widespread, but it exists. With some of the younger generation, there are cases in which the money is squandered. To the white friend and observer, it seems that something is taking place which is undermining sound standards and customs.

It is impossible for the Indian Service to take into account all of the details in a situation such as this, and federal laws are not drawn up with reference to all the contingencies that may arise, nor do they provide for a multitude of exceptions. Nevertheless, subtle harm can be done, which can break down a valuable part of Hopi character.

Sometimes the old standards hold out against temptations

with refreshing results. A Hopi who is past middle age was speaking to me of his wife's father. The old man must be over ninety, and not long ago he had an accident, which left him so badly crippled that he can get about only with great difficulty and only with the help of two stout canes. He is now quite unable to do any work or to contribute to his own support. The family considered the federal help that could be obtained, and decided against it. "We have always taken care of ourselves," my friend declared. "We have put our sons through school. It has not been easy, but we have managed. We had rather continue that way, and not take any money from the government."

The case of another Hopi friend of mine presents an illustration which is different but interesting. For many years he has been in government employment, in a somewhat minor capacity. His salary was not large enough to stimulate more than ordinary interest. Although he would presently be able to retire, his pension would be small. Consequently he felt that the job was not worth too much exertion; anyway his health was not good enough to warrant more than moderate activity. Then a revised schedule of salaries went into effect, and, on this basis, the prospective pension became substantially larger. Immediately my friend's standard of work stepped up, and his health became all right again.

In one vast aspect of human life, Western civilization has brought about no change in the thoughts and beliefs of the Hopis. After three hundred years of contact with the white race, they still believe that war is inherently and fundamentally wrong, that it should not be.

We of the white world, though deeply aware of the terrible character of war and its destructive consequences, believe that a time eventually comes when armed conflict is the only way to save ourselves from an evil that is greater than war itself. We know that this should not be the only way, but we feel that nothing else has been found which can effectively take its place, and we are convinced that we must sometimes resort to power. We believe that only through suppression of wrong can the world make progress.

There was a time, nearly three hundred years ago, when the ancestors of the Hopi people faced the obliteration of their beliefs, and, in desperation, adopted the one last way out. Their choice lay between the extinction of that which was the most vital part of their life and the destruction of the threatening force. They rose in rebellion and destroyed the enemy. Since that time, the Hopis have been faced with no similar alternative. They have been able to adhere to their conviction that violence is wrong. They sincerely and deeply believe that no good can come of war.

Inevitably the global conflicts of the last three decades have invaded Hopi life, though their beliefs have not been affected. On a living-room wall of a home which I visit there is a small picture of a young man in uniform. Above it is a tiny American flag. The boy was killed in one of the battles in Italy. Other Hopi homes saw sons set forth who never came back.

In a different way the after-effects of the last World War have also invaded Hopi life. Some of the men returning from that conflict brought back with them a taste for intoxicants. They came back from a different environment to a people in whom the belief has always prevailed that no man can rightly indulge in anything that can cause him to lose command of himself. In some instances the altered standards have spread to others and threaten to extend further. Many Hopis are concerned about this development. It represents an impact which they decry.

Probably all of us would agree that progress in the arts

should be one of the criteria of civilization. In some areas of art, the Hopis are proficient; in others they do not participate. Hopi women of First Mesa exhibit remarkable talent in the artistic forms they create in their pottery. This is in addition to their technical skill in handling clay and aside from the designs with which they decorate their pottery. A bowl or jar, as it takes shape under their hands, assumes curves and proportions which entitle it to rank high in the field of creative art. A number of Hopi men —a surprising number in relation to the total male population— have ability in pictorial art. They work in oils, in water colors, and in tempera. One of them, whom I visit, is increasingly called upon to do murals in churches. On the other hand, they are not at home with sculpture.

In the realm of music, the Hopis have nothing correspond-ing to our melodies and harmonies, our compositions, our instru-ments and orchestration. It is difficult for us to grasp and to ap-praise that which they enjoy. Yet they do have music and chants which to them are rewarding. Perhaps if our ears were attuned and our perceptions quickened, we would discover in their music a singular union of the imagery which their poetry captures and the rhythms and sequence of notes in which it is expressed. Per-haps, if we could see and hear as they do, we would find that their contribution, though very different from ours, is neverthe-less beautiful and significant.

NUMKE'NA

Among his younger friends, he is known as Sam. To older Hopis, he is Numke'na, which is pronounced Num-kee'-nah and which means "Warming at the fire." His age is in the neighborhood of eighty. Anyone who has visited Moenkopi has descended a hill in passing from the upper village to the lower. Sam Numke'-na's home overlooks the road and the hill. A wing of the house is built of adobe bricks—a rarity in the Hopi country.

WORDS AND PHRASES

V ERY FEW WHITE MEN indeed have ever achieved a mastery of the Hopi language. Probably the number can be counted on the fingers of your two hands, perhaps with some to spare. A trader may know and use various words and sentences, enough to transact business with an old Hopi who speaks no English, but not enough to carry on a real conversation. But the trader does not need to have a command of the language, since nearly all of the Hopi men, up to the age of sixty or beyond, speak English. Some of the men who are eighty or more attended school and learned to use the English language, speaking it perhaps slowly but adequately. As for the missionary, he is likely to use an interpreter who presumably can convey in Hopi idioms the content of a Bible verse or the missionary's injunctions.

To understand a sentence or a discussion that is spoken in Hopi is a very different matter from catching the meaning of a sentence spoken in French, for example. In the Hopi language there is nothing remotely familiar to the white man, nothing which he can grasp or surmise. Every noun, adjective, and verb is unfamiliar. There is no similarity, no clue. We have derived nothing in our language from the Hopi. Even a European language no longer spoken can be intelligible. *"Gallia est omnis divisa in*

The Hopis

partes tres" requires no profound mastery of Latin to comprehend what Caesar was saying.

Presumably Hopi is a difficult language. At least it gives that impression to one who has heard it spoken in many visits, has acquired a certain very limited vocabulary of common words and thereby learned that those words themselves can be tricky, has inquired concerning some phrases and discovered the subtle variations that apply to those phrases according to time and circumstances, has had a brief look at some Hopi verbs and learned that these follow no such rules as our own, has gained some glimpse of the imagery that may be found in the Hopi manner of expressing thought—all this without remotely approaching the ability to carry on any conversation in Hopi or even to speak a sentence.

In this experience also I learned that, among the Hopis, the command of the language varies widely with the individual. At first one assumes that a Hopi simply speaks Hopi, and that is all there is to the subject. As a matter of fact, an individual's command of his own tongue may be extensive, or it may be limited. He may have an exhaustive vocabulary and an exceptional facility of expression, or he may have only mediocre resources; the situation is no different from that which prevails in any other language.

The concept that a familiar English word conveys may have no parallel in any Hopi word. An interpreter may find it necessary to use a whole paragraph in Hopi in order to construct a picture which will make the English idea clear, drawing on related Hopi concepts and modifying them to fit the need. Similarly a single Hopi word is likely to denote details of meaning and to involve such connotation that a long clause or sentence or several sentences may be required to reproduce its meaning in English.

Words and Phrases

Since the Hopis have no written language, their words and sentences can be set down for us only in English characters, chosen to convey the sounds phonetically. This can be done reasonably well but leads to various difficulties.

The vowel sounds which we have they also have, but with some interesting and important variations. The vowel *a*, for example, is pronounced with a soft sound, much as we give it in the word *father*. But it may be prolonged, while remaining soft, as in the Hopi word for rabbit, *ta'bo,* pronounced *taah'boh,* or in the name of one of the Hopi villages, Ba'kabi, pronounced *Baah kahbee.* Sometimes the prolonged *a* changes completely the meaning of a word. Thus the Hopi word *ta'la* means a tassel, such as that of a corn plant, but if the first vowel is prolonged, so that the word is pronounced *taah'lah,* the meaning becomes "light"—any light, such as that of the sun. In a similar way, the word for a shrub, common in the mesa country, is *si'wi,* pronounced *see'wee,* but if you prolong the first syllable and make it *seee'wee,* you have the word for onion.

A vowel may be repeated in a word with a stop between. For example, the word for *my father* is *i'na a,* pronounced *ee'nah ah.* The word which means *I don't know* is Pi'i, pronounced *pee'ee.* The word for *piñon pine* is *tuve'e.* That for *my mother* is *i'ngu u,* pronounced *ee'ngoo-oo.*

In addition to the vowels familiar to us, the Hopis have a vowel which we cannot write with any English character and which has a sound somewhat like the French *eu*, though not quite the same.

When it comes to the consonants, the situation is again not simple. The consonants *f* and *v* are sometimes almost indistinguishable, and neither is quite like our own, because it is given with the lips only. The consonant *s* has a slight admixture of *h* in it. Where *n* appears in a word, it may be the same as ours or may have a *g* following it, so that it becomes *ng*, pronounced closely together, or may have the sound of *y*, closely following. The consonant *k̦* also may have *y* attached. Our combination *ch* may in some words sound more like *tc*, and our single letter *s*, at the beginning of a word, may become *ts*, as it does when you pronounce the name of the Hopi village Sicho′movi.

Immediately upon contact with the Hopis, the names of persons become interesting. Some of them are long names, and many end with similar syllables, frequently with—*tewa*. These endings have their descriptive meanings. Thus the ending—*quap′tewa* means something like *piled up on;*—*nimp′tewa* expresses the thought *entirely covered up*, and presumably refers to something which is round;—*wai′nim* is a feminine ending and means *walking;*—*tai′ma* conveys the idea of *looking for;*—*cho′-ma* means *a hill of* or *a heap of;*—*wy′tewa* signifies *running away* or *flying away;*—*yes′tewa* means settling down.

In the traditional Hopi practice, names of persons are descriptive. Every name is individualized; there is no family name such as we have. Sometimes a name which is the designation of a familiar animal, such as *Hona′ni*, the badger, is used by various families; but the possession of this name is not to be taken as necessarily indicating blood relationship. Sometimes in a family certain terminal syllables appear in the names of several members, perhaps because of a feeling of unity. The combination —*yes′tewa* was used by a family whom I know, along with various preliminary syllables, including *Pa-, Po′li-, Si′wi-,* and *Si′ki.*

In Hopi, various words are built, using a shortened form of some other word as a stem, offering interesting results in imagery, just as in our own English. For example, the Hopi word for *flower* or *plant* is *si′hu,* and the syllable used in word-building is *si*. The word for *red* is *pa la'*. The combination *sipa'la* becomes the word for *peach*. The word for *maiden* is *ma'na*, and from this the Hopis derive the word *man'si*, which designates the flower called the *Indian paintbrush*, literally *maiden flower*. The word for *child* is *tih*, and that for *seed* is *po'si*. This leads to the word *tipo'si*, which means *very small child* or *baby*. The Hopi word for *sun* is *ta'wa*, and from this comes *tawa'si*, literally *flower of the sun*, though it happens to be different from our own sunflower.

Another noun which plays an interesting part in Hopi word-building is the word for *house*, *ki'hu*, from which comes *ta'waki*, *sun house*, shortened to *ta'bki*, also *paho'ki*, the house where a *pa'ho* or *prayer offering* is deposited; we might call it a *shrine*. Perhaps from this same root is derived the word *ki'va*, the name of the traditional ceremonial chamber.

With the Hopis, as with us, the word that signifies a negative is combined with other words and reverses their meaning. The word *lo'loma* means *good, happy,* and *kalo'loma* means *ugly, bad*. The word *pe'te* means *heavy;* therefore *kape'te* means *light, not heavy*.

Sometimes the composite word gives us a glimpse into history. The ancient Hopi word for *squash* or *pumpkin* is *pa'ngna*. As certain varieties have been introduced, since the coming of the whites, modifying words have been added. One of the newer varieties is the *turban squash*. To the Hopis, this looked like the flat loaf of bread with a scalloped edge which they call *pika'viki*. So the *turban squash* was christened *pika'vik pa'ngna*.

In the Hopi world, salt was in use centuries before they had sugar. The word for *salt* is *oe'nga*. The word for *sweet* is *kwa'ngwa*. And so the phrase for sugar is *kwa'ngwa oe'nga, sweet salt*.

The Hopis

By natural extension of meaning, one word gives rise to another. In Hopi *hi'shaa* means *how long?* From this is derived *hi'shat,* meaning *ancient,* and from this comes *hi'shat paho'ki,* the designation for an *ancient shrine.*

One of the Hopi words signifying water, is *pa'hu,* which more accurately designates water as a natural phenomenon. From this word, various others are derived, such as *pa'tni, water jar; pavai'o, moisture; patu'bha, lake* or *ocean; pa'chua, water snake; pa'kwa, frog; pa'tki,* literally *water house* and the name of a clan; *pava'tiya, tadpole; pawi'ki, duck;* and *Tawa'pa, Sun spring.* Another, different word, *ku'yi,* connotes water in human use.

With some words, the form changes if the reference is to one, two, or several. Thus, the word for *friend* is *kwa'chi.* If I am referring to *my friend,* I say *ikwa'chi.* If *two friends* together are involved, the word becomes *na'kwachim,* with the *na-* given a prolonged sound. If the reference is to *several friends* together, the word is *na'nakwachim.*

Further complications arise from the custom which requires that a man use a different word, in some instances, from that which a woman uses for the very same purpose and under identical conditions. A man says *kwa'kwai'* for *thank you,* no matter whether he is addressing another man, a woman, or a mixed group. A woman always says *eskwa'li.* A man commenting on a beautiful flower uses the word *lo'loma,* but a woman uses the word *so'nwaiyo.*

In our language, in referring to various parts of a plant, such as corn, we customarily use two words, the plant name and that of the part to which we refer. We say corn ear, corn stalk, corn tassel. The Hopi is inclined to use distinctive words for the same purpose. *Ta'la* is *corn tassel; tala'si* is the pollen; *humi'ta* is the *shelled kernels; sa'mi* is the *unhusked corn; kutu'ki* is *parched corn kernels; tawa'kchi* is *sweet corn; pa'vunuvi* means *corn shoots* that are just coming through the ground; *pi'kya* is the *immature corn plant; ish'pi* is *corn that has been held over from a previous year; tu'oyi* is *corn that is corded up in a storehouse; tu'pebu* is *baked ears of sweet corn;* and *tu'moki* is a *bag for corn.*

In the Hopi language the generic word for bean is *mo'ri.* But where we would say *string beans, shell beans,* and so on, the Hopis are likely to have specific words. In Hopi, *string bean* is *pa'pu; shelled beans* are *mori'posi; Lima bean* is *hati'quo;* and a *single bean plant* is *muz'i.* With other desert plants, designations are specific. The *root of the narrow-leaved yucca* is *mo'vi;* the *top* is *mo'hu.* The *root of the broad-leaved yucca* is *sa'hu,* and the *top* is *samo'a.*

When it comes to verb forms in Hopi, the troubles of the white man really begin. The discovery soon is made that there are categories of verbs corresponding to such matters as stationary activities, positive actions, and innate qualities. There are various prefixes and suffixes which have much to do with the function and meaning of verbs. Other complexities exist that lead the visitor to wonder how any white man, even though he were to live for a long time with the Hopi people seeking to acquire a mastery of the language, could achieve proficiency.

For example, a Hopi verb, when used with a singular object, may be quite different from the form required with a plural object. The verb meaning *to carry, to take along,* for example, is *ya'wma,* in the first instance, but becomes *ki'ma,* in the second. The object of the verb brings about the difference. The verb meaning *to give* is *ma'ka,* if the object of the giving is singular, but *he'yta,* if plural. Here again the change in form is brought about by the plurality of the object of the verb, not by that of the

HONA'NI

Slight in build, he is none the less active and is always
genial and responsive. He is the youngest of the living
grandsons of old Tuba, who was a leader in his day.
Hona'ni's name, pronounced Hoh-nah'-nee, means
"Badger." His comfortable home is in the far end of
Lower Moenkopi, adjoining that of Doyo'uma's, his
brother-in-law. His age is about eighty.

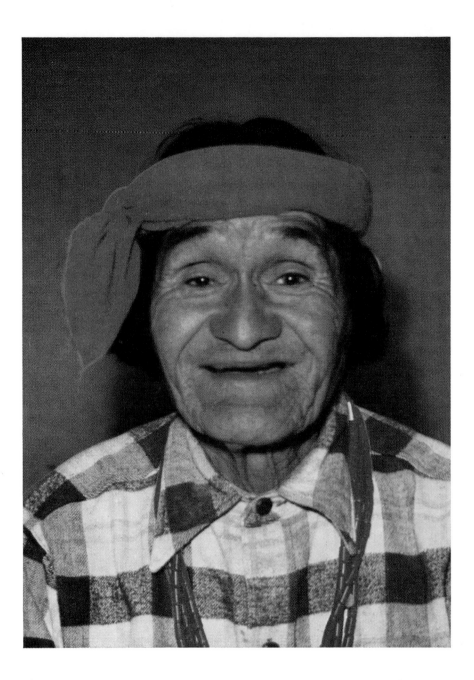

subject as one might expect. *To toss* a single object is *te'va,* but *to toss* or *throw* several objects is *ma'spa.* On the other hand, the verb to *sit* is *ka'te* in the case of a singular subject, but it becomes *ye'se* if the subject is more than one.

From the earliest light before sunrise, on through the day to the darkness of night, the old Hopi custom designated the successive stages in a series of descriptive words and phrases, based on the position of the sun. Although you could not have timed the arrival and departure of trains by this system, it nevertheless had its advantages. By our accustomed plan, six o'clock in the morning, in summer, is different in character from six in winter. In the Hopi plan, differences are eliminated. Also, a man always had his "clock" with him, perpetually wound and ready for use.

The very earliest light, the first indication of approaching dawn, is designated *kucha'nuptu,* the *white dawn,* literally *the white is arising.* Soon afterwards, as colors begin to suffuse the sky, the phrase is *sikya'nuptu,* the *yellow dawn.* Then, as the sun begins to appear, the hour is *ta'wa ya'ma, the sun comes out.*

The whole period from the first beginning of light until the sun has made its appearance is sometimes spoken of as *tala'vaiyi,* the period when the sky is *painted with light.* A Hopi may look upon this array and address it with the words *Lo'loma tala'vaiyi!*

When the sun has fully cleared the horizon, the descriptive words are *ta'wa ove'e, the sun is up.* When it has climbed an appreciable distance toward the zenith, the expression is *tu u'nava,* because there is sunshine all about. When noon arrives, the phrase is *ta'wa na'shabi,* which means *the sun is midway in its course.*

As the afternoon moves along and the sun begins its long descent toward the horizon, the descriptive word is *ha'yoma,* derived from *descending.* Later, as the sun approaches the horizon, it is spoken of as *drawing near to his house, ta'wa apa'bi ki'-hu,* or in shortened form, simply *ta'bki.* As it begins to set, or as the Hopis say, *to enter,* the expression is *ta'wa paki'to;* and, when the last of the glowing disk has disappeared, *ta'wa pa'ki—the sun has gone in.*

Twilight is *ta'shubi,* derived from the words *ta'wa shulau'ti,* meaning *there is no longer any sun.* As the twilight fades into darkness, the word *ma'si, gray,* appears in the expression *masi'-phi.* Then comes *mi'hi, night,* and at *midnight* the phrase *to kil'na sha'ptu.*

The Hopis seem not to make use of any expression corresponding to our *Hello!* or *How do you do!* If you meet a man walking along the road, you may say *Um pu ni'man?—Are you on your way home?—*or *Um haka'mi?—Where are you going?* But these are genuine questions as well as greetings. As a Hopi friend explained to me, "With our people a man may often be alone. Maybe he is going out to herd sheep for several days. Maybe he is on his way to his field somewhere. It is wise to know where he is going. Then if he should be needed, or if anything should happen, we'd know where to look for him."

When you knock on the door of a Hopi home, someone inside, presumably the owner of the home, will say *"Pe'o ia'a,"* *"Come in!"* But this has a connotation which goes beyond the mere invitation to enter. In derivation, it refers both to you, the visible person standing there, and to an invisible spirit beside you. It means that more than one is invited to enter. After you have opened the door, a further greeting is spoken by the one inside, probably *"Ie'se e,"* which again welcomes both you and the unseen guest, the invisible spirit with you. When a chair has been placed for you, the invitation to be seated is expressed in words which refer only to you, the guest in person, but up to that point

226

Words and Phrases

the traditional greeting includes that ever-present concept of the Hopi people, the spirit that is a companion and a part of every creature.

An old Hopi friend, the companion of many expeditions and many talks together, was explaining for me the meaning of various Hopi words and phrases.

"What about the word *kuyiva'to?*" I asked.

"That is a prayer," he said. "Early in the morning when dawn is coming, even while it is still dark and before there is any light in the sky, you stand and look toward the east. You must be silent and you must be worshipful. While you watch the light coming you say a prayer, just to yourself. That is *kuyiva'to.*"

GLIMPSES

"IT IS BETTER for the Hopis not to have a written language," said my Hopi friend. "Better for their religion and their beliefs."

He went on to explain. "When a religion is written down it gets into unfriendly hands. A man who does not understand reads it and criticizes it. He says that it is wrong, and there is nobody with him to explain and help him to understand. Another man comes along and changes something. He writes it out with the changes in it that he has added, and that starts something different from what it was intended to be. Then after a while somebody else reads what the last man has written, and he says 'No. That man wasn't right. This is the way it ought to be.' So he sets to work and writes something else. Then all these different people begin to argue and quarrel. Each one thinks that he is right and that all the others are wrong.

"We believe that this is what has been going on all over the world. It is too bad that this is so, because it sets people against each other. Their religion does not help them the way it should. It makes them unhappy. Sometimes they even fight about it.

"With the Hopis the rules and beliefs are spoken, not written down. An older man gives the instructions to a younger man. He

228

holds his mouth close to the younger man's ear and tells him the Hopi truths, just as he was taught them by his own father or grandfather. He had to learn them exactly right when he was young, because that has always been the rule. When he tells them to the younger man he repeats them, over and over. The younger man must do the same until he knows them so well that he will never make a mistake and will never forget them, no matter where he is or what he is doing. When he is older he will repeat them to his own son or grandson. He will always remember them.

"That is the way it has been with the Hopis for hundreds of years. We think that it is the better way."

Whatever food you have brought into a house in the afternoon or evening must remain there overnight. If you have dropped crumbs on the floor as you ate your evening meal, they must not be swept out of the door that night. Hova'kpi explained the rule.

"All these things," he said, "are the gifts of the Great Power. They are something which the Power has created. They must be honored. If any of them were swept out of the door when night comes, they would be dishonored. The right way to do is to allow everything to remain in the house through the night, because in that way the gifts share the house with you, just like your children. Then in the morning you may gather things up or sweep up the floor and carry things outside—not throw them out."

In the course of most ceremonies the period arrives when gifts are distributed to those who are looking on. Perhaps the gifts are small—slices of bread, pieces of melon—nevertheless, men go about bestowing something on everyone. Bread is tossed individually to boys and men seated on the roof of bordering dwellings; other gifts are handed to women and children in doorways and windows. The custom is all-inclusive and inviolate.

In various ceremonies paints for the decorations applied to face and body of the participants are essential. The Hopis have learned how to make these through long experience.

A combination of sumac berries and boiled purple corn, crushed and mixed with white clay, provides a purple paint. Charcoal, combined with chewed melon seeds, with water added, provides another. White clay alone often decorates the face and body. The petals of sunflowers, dried and powdered, mixed with yellow corn meal, produce a face powder used by women in the Basket Dance. Clowns use the yellow berries of a small gray-green plant for beads. Desert flowers provide red or green stains. Powdered shale is a source of black decorations. The flowers of rabbit brush, boiled down with an earth deposit, give a thick yellow paint.

There is an interesting parallel between an impressive rite performed in one of the major Hopi ceremonies and a drama that was enacted by the ancient Celtic people. A vast gulf of space and time separates the two peoples, but each has developed a similar concept that is symbolized in much the same way.

The Hopi ceremony is the one which they call the *Wu'wuch-im*. It is long and elaborate, marked by many detailed acts. In certain years it includes the traditional initiation rituals in which young men are admitted to adult status—a drama of which the white visitor to the reservation may become aware because all roads and trails into a village are strictly barred.

Glimpses

Early in the course of the *Wu'wuchim* the rite of the *new fire* is enacted. In every Hopi home every fire of any kind is extinguished. The home is closed from any contact with any other part of the village. All the women and children of the household must remain strictly secluded within the four walls. In each of the kivas, also, every trace of fire, every spark or glowing coal, is obliterated. Thus, the concept of death before rebirth is symbolized.

Then in the kiva, wherein the heart of the ceremony takes place, one of the leaders takes up a fire drill and begins twirling it in the base provided for it. In a few minutes, his tinder of dry cedar bark is alight. The fire is nursed, more cedar is added, and soon the *new fire* is strong and ready. Messengers carry flaming brands to the other kivas, where fuel awaits their coming. Then from the various kivas, brands are carried to the homes. And thus new birth—the coming of new life, the creation after the darkness of death—is made vivid.

The *Wu'wuchim* is celebrated in November, as was the ancient Celtic ritual. With the Celtic people the first of November marked the beginning of a new year, and this ceremony celebrated its coming. In the course of the Celtic ritual, all fires in all the homes were extinguished, symbolizing the death of evil. A great fire was then built in the open, and brands from this were carried to the homes, signifying for each household its participation in the rebirth.

The details of Hopi rituals are specific and exacting. A little sprig of the plant that they call *bam'navi* is bound near the base of a prayer stick. It is one of the group of plants that we call snakeweed. But it must be this particular one. The right kind is the "female" and only the female can serve.

231

DOYO'UMA

He lives in almost the very last house toward the south, in the village of Lower Moenkopi. A part of the house is old, with sunken metates and with anchor rings for a loom. The other part is new, with smoothly-plastered walls. Doyo'uma has lived there since his marriage, a long time ago. He is now about eighty years old. His name means "Admired." It is pronounced Doh-yoh'-oo-mah.

Glimpses

A Hopi woman today who is about to have a baby is likely to go to a hospital to have it. But she and other Hopi women have not forgotten a traditional rule concerning the first three weeks after the birth of a child. A Hopi friend told me about this and the reason for the rule's coming into being.

"If you plant a seed in the ground," he said, "it will be about ten days before the little plant first shows above the surface. Sometimes a little less, sometimes a little more. But about ten days.

"The plant as it first appears, though, is not just like it will be a little later. It does not yet have the right leaves. Its shape is not right. It has made a start, and if it can live and grow a little more and not suffer any harm, it will be the way it ought to be. But it must be protected. The hot sun must not shine on it while it is so little and tender. Otherwise it may die.

"Another ten days are necessary, so that it may gain strength. At the end of that time it will still be only a little plant, but it will be like it is going to be as it grows larger. It will have the kind of leaves that are right for it. It will not be harmed if the sun shines on it.

"A baby is like a plant that has started to grow from a seed. It must be protected in just the same way. It needs the ten days that were required while the seed was sending the little plant up to the surface of the ground, and the other ten days while the right leaves were forming. For twenty days the sun must not shine on it. Then on the twenty-first day its mother takes it in her arms and, along with her mother or some other woman, carries it out of the house to the edge of the mesa and there prays for its health and happiness. On that day the baby is given its name.

"This," he added, "is the reason why the windows of a house are covered where a baby has just been born."

The Hopis

During the twenty days that a newborn baby remains within the house shielded from any sunlight, the father's side of the family may have a traditional task to perform. In some communities it is the custom for the father or grandfather to weave a blanket for the baby, especially if it is a boy—a soft, warm square, done in broad white and black bars, or brown and white, forming a checkered pattern. I have seen and handled such a blanket, woven many years ago and used by the family ever since. Its distinctive pattern, fixed by ancient custom, easily identifies it.

My white friend, Shine, companion of many a trip, likes to drive an ancient "Chevy" coupe. In it he is a familiar and loved figure in the mesa country. Sometimes he visits a Hopi village, and then the children flock to his car, calling him by a nickname that they have given him, responding enthusiastically to his greeting, climbing all over the car, and blocking the open windows with their laughing faces. I can testify to this, because more than once we have been obliged to move along in order to clear the windows and get a breath of air.

Not long ago Shine drove into a village and left his car while he called on a friend. When he caught sight of the coupe on his way back, he saw that it was literally covered with youngsters, little children five or six years old, others seven or eight. They were on the hood of the car, on the running board, and on the top. He paused to count them. There were fifteen.

Then he discovered that they were reciting something together, in perfect unison, soberly, without hesitation, and without a break.

" 'The world will little note nor long remember . . . that we here highly resolve . . .' " And steadily on to the end of Lincoln's immortal address, " ' . . . and that government of the people, by the people, for the people, shall not perish from the earth.' "

On a wall in Ho'ko's house hangs a small, flat oblong of wood, measuring perhaps three or four inches wide and five or six inches long. Its surface is decorated with a simple symbolic design, and a small feather is attached to its upper margin. It is a Kachina which once was laid before an eagle on the day before the captive was sacrificed. It was made by Ho'ko's great-grandfather, and has been carefully preserved ever since.

"He was over ninety years old when he made it," Ho'ko says. "It is hung up there so that it will not be harmed."

Ba'toti is a very old man. Members of his family tell me that he is either ninety-seven or ninety-eight. A neighbor who himself is in his eighties was inclined to be doubtful when I spoke of Ba'toti's age, but the neighbor, like many another old person, is given to doubts in a matter which involves the age of some one else. The family feel that their information is reliable.

Certainly Ba'toti is old. He walks now with a cane; his hearing is impaired; and his eyes are none too good. But the usual characteristics of old age stop there. In spirit he is as alert as ever. He is erect; he does not flinch at an ice-cold bath; he is ready to undertake any activity that he could conceivably perform; and he would like to undertake many things that he could not conceivably perform. If younger members of his family are about to embark on some enterprise, he sees no reason why he should not do likewise.

Recently he was visiting a son in southern Arizona. At that time cotton picking was in full swing, and the son's family took advantage of the opportunity to pick cotton for a neighbor, at so much a pound. I happened to visit the family the evening after this activity began.

It developed that Ba'toti was determined not to be denied taking part in the cotton-picking. He had insisted on going along. Reluctantly, they assigned him a place on a row of cotton, provided him with a bag, and let him have his way.

At first in his picking he delayed repeatedly to clean the trash from each boll and even to remove the seed before he deposited the boll in his bag. That is the procedure in which he had been trained as a boy in the small cotton field attached to his family's land in the Hopi reservation. After a while, the others discovered what he was doing and told him that the gin would take care of all that. The idea was new, for there had been no cotton gin in his youth, but, with some protest, he acquiesced.

His delay in cleaning each boll cut down his total for the day. But when they checked up at the end of the day, Ba'toti turned in ninety-one pounds of cotton.

When I saw him that evening, he was at least as fresh and wide-awake as the younger members of the family. In fact, I think, rather more so.

Seldom, if ever, do you see a Hopi man smoking a pipe. But pipes are owned; they are smoked in the kivas, and sometimes by older men in the seclusion of their homes.

Wild tobacco grows in the Hopi country—*pi'va* they call it— a plant with smaller and narrower leaves than those of our cultivated tobacco. It is in demand for ceremonial use and is not abundant enough to meet those needs readily. Sometimes men make long trips, perhaps a hundred miles, to secure a supply. Any part of it that they do not need themselves they can easily sell.

238

Glimpses

Kwa'ni is the leader of one of the great ceremonies in the village in which he lives. For three decades he has occupied that position, and, for many years before that, he filled the position that is next in importance. Before that, ever since his initiation, he was trained in the multitude of details involved in that ceremony —the long series of acts in the drama, the precise manner of performing each detail in each act, the exact phraseology used in the spoken words. Perhaps a white man who has risen to the highest honors in Masonry would find in his own experience some parallel to the requirements that Kwa'ni was obliged to meet.

Kwa'ni is also one of the spiritual leaders of the people in his village. This accompanies his leadership in the ceremony. It would be wrong to conclude that his ceremonial position confers the other status; rather, the two go hand in hand.

In his daily life Kwa'ni has followed the traditional Hopi precepts. He could not have done otherwise and still have attained the position which he occupies. For him all living things have their place in the world; all have a spiritual aspect as well as a physical one; and all are the manifestations of what he thinks of as a Great Power, just as the sun, the moon, and the stars, the rain, the snow, and the earth itself are similar manifestations. This is never to be forgotten. The obligations that arise from this belief are never to be slighted.

Once it happened that Kwa'ni was spending a few days with relatives, in a region far from the Hopi country. It happened, also, that I was visiting in that same area. There, a shrub known as arrowweed grows abundantly. We would not naturally call it a weed, for it is woody, with straight and slender branches, and it grows to a height of ten feet or more. The rigid branches have long been used by the Indians for arrow shafts. They serve another use, also, in the hands of those who know how to utilize

239

them. A straight branch, about a half-inch in diameter, cut to a length of eighteen or twenty inches and smoothly rounded on the end, becomes a fire drill, a means of making fire by friction. It is a valuable adjunct in ceremonies.

When I ran across Kwa'ni he was on his way to a clump of arrowweed, and I walked along with him. The branches of the shrub grew tall and straight; they would make good fire drills, and there was an ample supply of them.

Kwa'ni selected a plant, but before he got out his knife and opened its sharp blade he did something else. From a pocket he drew a small buckskin bag, untied its string, and took from it some of the cornmeal which it contained—the sacred meal of the Hopis. Silently, he scattered this over the shrub.

He was about to destroy life, only that of a common plant, which grew in countless numbers, but he could not do even that without a silent prayer.

In the old Hopi belief there is never a time when a prayer, spoken silently and alone, should be forgotten.

We were spending the evening in Kwa'ni's home, talking with him and with his son. The hour was growing late and the old man was tired and ready for bed. He excused himself, walked to the open door, and stood for a moment under the stars.

"All his life," said his son, "he has done that. He always prays before he goes to bed. He never forgets."

"Do you know about the silent name?" Siva'pi inquired. I asked him to tell me about it.

"Well, when a man passes away, first of all his hair is washed in yucca suds. This is to prepare him for his journey. It means that he has been purified and that his spirit is made ready for the place where it will go. The man's father's sister does this for him.

240

If she is no longer living, some other female relative serves as his attendant.

"Then his face is rubbed with white cornmeal, so that it may be like the face of a spirit. After that, a mask of white cotton is placed over his face. This is like a cloud and represents his soul. Then the attendant fastens around his forehead a cotton string with feathers attached, which hang down over his face. There are four of these feathers, and they are the symbols of his life. If he has been a leader of his people, the feathers chosen will be especially long and will honor him for following the Hopi way and having a good heart.

"When all this has been done, the attendant stands before him and addresses him. 'You have completed this life,' she says. 'Now you are going to your new home, where you will be with many others that you have known here, and where you will be happy. You have been known here by the name that was given you at your initiation. You will not use that name any more. You will leave that here with your body because you will not have any more need for it. In your new home you will have a new name. Your name will be———.

"But the attendant does not speak the name. She only thinks it. The spirit of the man knows what it is, but no one else ever knows.

"That is the silent name."

"Why," asked a white visitor, "do the Hopis always bury a deceased person in a sitting position?"

"You see," explained Siva′pi, "the person who has passed along must be ready for the journey to his new home. He must face the east because that is where the sun rises. He must be ready to get up quickly. So his body must be placed in a sitting position

MARGARET

She is a granddaughter of Siwiquap'tewa (Seba James). Although only four years old, she knows how to do her part in household duties.

and it must face toward the right direction. Then his spirit can rise quickly when the right time comes."

Smoke, as the older Hopis think of it, can be a cleansing and purifying agent. There are times when it should be used for that purpose. The burial of one who has died is such an occasion. The persons who have taken part in the burial have had to deal with a body which is no longer living but is now abandoned by the spirit of the one who has lived in it. It is best that these persons be purified. One of the ways to do this is to burn some piñon gum and let the smoke cover them. That way they will be cleansed and ready to resume their daily lives.

Visiting with some Hopi friends one evening, I brought up the subject of superstitions. One might suspect that among the Hopi people, living as they do, close to nature and in circumstances where good luck or bad might play a considerable part in personal fortunes, a belief in portents would flourish. I wished to learn whether any of the common superstitions of our own race has any parallel in Hopi ideas.

I found that my friends had no reservations about the number 13. This was not unexpected, since the origin of our superstition is supposed to trace back to an event in Norse mythology, the banquet of the twelve gods at Valhalla, where a thirteenth spirit, the spirit of discord, entered uninvited. Nor had my friends any special regard for the number 7, that potent number which bestows supernatural powers on the seventh son of the seventh son.

However, they do look upon the number 4 as significant. There are four compass directions. The kiva has four walls. In many rituals, an act is performed four times. This is the vital number, the one that signifies completeness. If anything is especially important, it should have the benefit of four enactments.

Friday, I found also, has no special significance. This again was not unexpected, since the distrust of this day, its unhappy place among the days of the week, is believed to be derived from the account of the Crucifixion, and this event in history is not in the Hopi religion.

I spoke of some lesser portents that appear widely in superstitions of the white race: the broken mirror which is supposed to bring bad luck—an omen presumed to date back to remote times when the reflection in a small pool of water was conceived of as the soul and a disturbance of the reflection was thought to harm the soul; the spilled salt, which even Leonardo da Vinci used in his painting "The Last Supper"; or the almost universal black cat, dating back to the times of ancient Egypt. None of these, I found, has any parallel in the Hopi beliefs.

How about the rainbow? Is that a sign of good fortune to come? No, the rainbow is a barrier. The rain that is falling on the other side cannot pass through and reach the place where those who see the rainbow are standing—a belief which probably is drawn from hard experience.

In many parts of the world special properties have been attached to the ashes left from the burning of sacred objects, such as the consecrated palms used in some religious ceremonies in Europe. Mixed with seeds intended for planting, these ashes are presumed to insure abundant crops. In much more remote times, animals were sacrificed, their bodies burned, and the ashes scattered on the fields. Among the Hopis the importance of ashes finds a parallel. In the kiva, at a time of ceremony, a fire is kept burning, using certain specified wood as fuel—greasewood, sumac, saltbush, or rabbit brush. Ashes from these fires have special significance and are used subsequently in the planting of seeds and the prayers for crops.

I found no parallel to the belief so widely prevalent in various other countries that a stone of unusual shape or history may possess extraordinary properties. In many regions the belief has prevailed that a certain stone has been credited with healing, conferring good fortune, or warding off evil. Especially a stone with a natural hole through its center has been considered a talisman. Over this my friends were amused. "Why," they exclaimed, "should a stone with a hole in it have any power?"

They were still more amused when I spoke of other superstitions. The fact that a rabbit is born with its eyes open and, according to superstition, can therefore see unfortunate events before they happen had no appeal. The notion that the foot of a rabbit, carried in the pocket, can warn the owner seemed to my friends just foolish.

They laughed when I spoke of other notions from the white man's collection: if you get out of bed on the wrong side you will have bad luck, the wrong side being the opposite one from that which you used in going to bed; if you button up your jacket the wrong way you must take it off and start over; if, in putting on your coat, you insert the left arm first, instead of the right, you will have trouble all day; if you enter a house with your left foot first, instead of your right, something will happen to you; if your right ear burns, someone is speaking well of you, but, if it is your left ear, someone is speaking ill of you—a notion that was held by the ancient Greeks and used by Shakespeare; if you see the new moon over your right shoulder, you will be lucky; if you see a pin on the floor and pick it up, you will have good fortune, provided the point of the pin is directed away from you. All this gave my friends much amusement.

247

The Hopis

"Talk about the Indian being superstitious!" they exclaimed. "How about the white man!"

The practice of spitting on your bait for good luck has a venerable history. When you perform this rite you are giving of your own body, and therein lies its potency. Two thousand years ago, a somewhat similar practice was followed to ward off harm or to insure a desired end. Among the Hopis the idea is suggested in some details associated with their sacred rituals. So far as I know, however, it does not play a part in ordinary activities.

The superstition, also, of touching wood, as a measure for avoiding ill effects that might result from boasting, dates back to antiquity, to the times when spirits were personified in trees. From that came the belief that such objects as the wooden doors of churches represent the same guardian spirits. Seemingly, this belief does not exist among the Hopi people.

When I asked my Hopi friends about the belief that a bride should be carried over the threshold of her home by her husband, their comment was a laughing reminder that a Hopi bride could not very well be carried in anyone's arms, dressed as she is in her wedding robes and carrying across her arms a reed roll containing part of her wedding costume. As for the shoe thrown for good luck, based though it is on ancient tradition, again the Hopis have no corresponding custom.

The Hopi people are not given to predicting future events from chance happenings. The birds that fly across the road from right to left, instead of straight ahead, or from left to right, do not portend disaster. A man does not expect accidents to happen just because the beans are in flower. He does not carry a magic stone in his pocket. Perhaps, for the Hopis, future events are too important to be brought to pass or averted by trifles. The future is a matter for prayer, rather than the reading of omens in stones.

Glimpses

In China, it is said, the tortoise is regarded as a symbol of long life. The pattern of the markings on its shell can be studied and, from these markings, details of the future can be divined. Among the Hopis, the shell of a turtle is prized because it forms the rattle used in ceremonies. The rattle, because of its religious use, becomes a sacred object, but there seems to be no thought of ascribing to its markings any key to the future.

A ceremony in the plaza is an occasion for prolonged baking activities on the part of the women of a village.

In Mishong'novi, the final act of the *Niman* was under way. Through much of the morning, women were making trips to a part of the mesa that offers seclusion, hidden from the village by vertical rocks. They went singly and by two and threes, carrying bulky bundles, done up in spotless white, big trays, and baskets covered with snowy cloths.

At noon, when there was an intermission, the men in their ceremonial costumes filed into the area, removed their elaborate headdresses, placed them carefully in a row along the edge of the mesa, and transferred their kilts to crevices in the vertical rocks. Traditional food awaited them. Piled up on white cloths was a heap of blue piki that would have filled a wagon, every feather-light roll of it made from cornmeal hand-ground on metates and hand-baked on piki stones. Shouldering these, were loaves of bread, a great mound of them, baked in outdoor ovens. There was much more food then the men could eat, but they did their best.

To the Hopis the performances of the clowns who invade a ceremony in a plaza are well understood. The grotesque figures may imitate both the costumes and the rituals of the participants

249

in the drama. Sometimes they try to interfere. They may invent songs and make loud noises. In the midst of a beautiful passage in the ritual, they may try to interrupt with a brazen imitation.

In spite of all this the real drama does not falter. Its intent is too important, its symbolism too real, its place in Hopi prayers too secure to suffer any harm. The ribald clowns, loud and insistent as they often are, cannot prevail against the ancient Hopi ritual and the concepts which it signifies.

Sixty years ago, Alexander M. Stephen, observing the Buffalo Dance at Walpi, wrote, "There is an utter absence of affectation in the dancers . . . In their exhibitions in public their every thought seems to be given to the dancing and posturing *per se*, not to any effect they make as individuals."

Watching the same dance in Shungo'pavi this year, I had the same impression. The Dance has various acts, and they are all vigorous. They involve specific movements of hands and feet, as well as the patterns woven by the dancers. Some of the participants were young folk, and they gave complete attention to the correct rendering of their parts, like animated figures.

The calm and self-possession of a Hopi in the presence of a rattlesnake seems never-failing. Apparently it is not restricted to the performance of the priests in the Snake ceremony. One might almost conclude that between the snake and the man there is some sort of private understanding.

Mo'vi was gathering up corn fodder in his field one day. His land is situated in a low-lying area where rattlesnakes are by no means uncommon. Seemingly, they like the occasional shade, and probably their food is more abundant there than on the open mesa.

250

Glimpses

The cornstalks were lying in heaps. Mo′vi encircled one of these with his arms and lifted it waist high. As he did so, there was a warning whir from within the heap. Any one of us would have thrown the heap from him as far as he could and probably would have jumped back in fright. Mo′vi did nothing of the sort. Gently and carefully he replaced the heap of fodder on the ground. If the rattler were reassured, it would do no harm.

For many a generation the old Hopi custom has prescribed that a boy must be trained so that he will develop physical vigor. He must be strong of limb, sound of wind, and able to endure heat and cold. In some of the ceremonies, he must go through his part outdoors, in midwinter, stripped to a breechcloth and moccasins. In others, in the heat of midsummer, he must continue for a long time a performance in which he wears a heavy costume, with head and neck sometimes enclosed in a thick mask. At any time of year, in his ordinary pursuits, he must be capable of duties which sometimes require exceptional physical endurance. In the desert country, a man may work alone all day or for several days, beyond the reach of help and in an environment that can be pitiless. The time may come when a man's survival depends solely on his strength.

The field where Na′qua raises his corn is situated eight miles from the village in which he lives. No road that a car can follow leads to it. To reach it, you may use horses and a wagon, you may go on horseback, or you may travel on foot. Most of the time, Na′qua goes on horseback.

It was early July and very hot. In late afternoon Na′qua rode his horse to his field, planning to cultivate his corn the next day. Since he would be coming back the following afternoon, he took no provisions, other than five or six cylinders of piki, done up in a big handkerchief tied to his belt. He already had a small melon stowed away at the field. That and the piki would make a good supper.

The small shelter that he maintains at the field provided his overnight lodging. In the early morning, when the white glow in the east was changing to the yellow of dawn, Na'qua arose, ready to begin his day's work. He had tethered his horse in a little hollow where there is a cottonwood tree. His first glance in that direction told him that something was wrong. His horse was gone. The broken end of a rope, still tied to the tree, gave him the rest of the story.

The tracks that had been left by the horse and the trailing rope led off toward the south, away from home. Na'qua hurried to a little rise from which he could scan the vast expanse of desert in that direction. There was no sign of his mount. He examined the tracks carefully. Although a light breeze was blowing, it had not yet moved any of the fine grains of sand into the tracks. He reasoned that the horse could not have been gone more than an hour. The spacing of the tracks readily informed him that the animal was moving at an easy gait, not a walk, but not a run.

The sun climbing over the horizon was already sending warmth across the desert, and this would soon increase into the blazing heat of July. Na'qua quickly removed his trousers and stowed them in his shelter. He peeled off his shirt and tied it around his waist. Although the horse had an hour's start, he could catch up with the animal. Na'qua set out in a steady run.

For the most part, the tracks were not difficult to follow. They were a little obscure where they crossed stony stretches, but it was easy to run there. They were plain enough where the desert was sandy, but across those places the running was not so easy.

As the sun rose higher and its heat increased, perspiration

began to drip from Na′qua's face and body. That was to be expected, and he gave it no thought. He must surely be gaining on the horse. The tracks showed no change, only a steady moderate gait. Quite likely the animal would stop pretty soon to feed on the sparse grass that grew in some places. Once his pursuer had caught up with him, the rest would be easy.

A low hill not far from the tracks tempted him. He diverged and hurried to its higher ground to search the desert to the south. Far off he thought that he could make out a little speck, too far off to be sure, but it was encouraging. He resumed his running pursuit.

Two hours passed. Three hours. It seemed as if the tracks were a little sharper. He must be gaining on the beast. Four hours. The perspiration was running from him now in earnest. Five hours.

He was not hungry but he was very thirsty. He wished that he had filled his water bottle and brought it along. A little water now and then would be pretty good in all that heat. He could have filled the bottle, for there is a small spring within walking distance of the cornfield. But it takes time to fill a bottle there, for there is only a little trickle of water, especially in July. It takes time to go to the spring. If he had done that, he would have lost half an hour. Then he would never have caught up with the horse. It was better not to have delayed.

But he was very thirsty.

Six hours. The sun was almost directly overhead. Seven hours.

And then Na′qua came to a place where the tracks diverged on a sandy trail which he knew led to a far-off crossing of the Little Colorado's dry bed, and on to the still more distant place

where he had bought the horse. There was no use in going any
farther. He knew the place where the tracks diverged, knew that
it was forty miles from his home. He also knew that he must
now backtrack. He could follow a little more direct line on his
return, but it was still more than thirty miles. At a steady walk
now, intsead of a run, he set out.

Slowly the sun moved toward the west. Na'qua welcomed
this, because he knew that, in time, the heat would diminish.
But, after he had been traveling another two hours, he also
knew that his thirst was telling on him. He could not make it
home unless he could get some water.

Out of his knowledge of the country he recalled a shallow
wash where sometimes animals pawed down through the sand
and found moisture. He set out in the direction in which the wash
ought to be, and half-an-hour later he found it. Down in its bed
he dug in the sand, waited for the shallow hollow slowly to fill,
and managed to drink some of the brownish liquid. The water
was bitter. It gave nim some of the moisture that he needed, but
it did little to satisfy his thirst.

He knew that somehow he had to get more water as he continued his walk toward home. Again, his knowledge of the
country came to his rescue. Farther down the wash, there was a
place where sometimes a Navajo family crossed it, and sometimes
stopped to rest their horses. At such a place, they might also eat
some food, might open a can of tomatoes and leave the empty
can. If they had done so, and if he could find the can, he could
use it to carry water with him through the rest of his journey.
On this slim possibility he set out down the wash.

At the end of a slow and hard mile he came to the crossing.
Almost buried in the sand he found the can that he sought. Again

he plodded another hard mile up the wash. He dug further in the hollow that he had made and waited a long half hour while it slowly filled. He filled his precious tomato can only halfway, since any more would only be lost as he carried it with him.

The sun was touching the horizon as he set out from the wash. An hour later, its burning heat had given way to the chill of the desert night. Although he had only a shirt with him for clothing, Na'qua did not mind the sudden drop in temperature. That which did give him concern was his growing exhaustion. He knew that fifteen miles still lay ahead of him and for the first time he began to doubt whether he could make it. His thirst also was insistent. Every once in a while he sipped a little water from the can, no more than a spoonful; while this was better than nothing, it was far from adequate.

At the end of an hour he had covered a mile and a half. In another hour, only another mile. Although there was no moon, he could see well enough by starlight to follow the right course. Increasingly, he found it necessary to rest. Twice he lay down for a few minutes, though he did not permit his eyes to close. His exhaustion was now so evident that his doubt about the outcome became almost a certainty. In another hour, he realized that he had gained no more than a half mile.

Then for the third time, his knowledge of the desert came to his aid. Far off to the left, perhaps two miles away, stood a small shelter, occupied at times by a herder taking care of sheep. There was a chance that someone might be staying there for the night. The walk to it would take all his remaining strength and might be fruitless, but the distance to his own place was far greater and had clearly become impossible to cover. He turned and started off.

The Hopis

Most of his course now lay over level ground, which offered a welcome hard surface. He managed this part without too much increase of exhaustion. The fact that he was headed toward a nearer objective seemed to give him some renewed strength. But the last half mile was different. Here there were three sandy ridges that had to be crossed. There was no way around. Painfully he struggled over the first and the second of these. The slope that led up the third seemed to take every ounce of strength that he had left. He made the last few yards on his hands and knees, and lay completely exhausted on the top. The realization came to him that this must be the end.

Lying there, he became dimly aware of the fact that down below a dog was barking. Again on his hands and knees, he fought his way through the sand, down the slope, and across the space to the shelter.

A moment later someone picked him up and carried him inside.

He had won.

TRANSITION

Ever since the beginnings of community existence among the people we call the Hopis some change in the manner of life must have been going on. Alterations in climate alone would bring this about, as would the development of a new crop, the decrease in game, the unfortunate erosion of a valley floor, the rise and decline of a craft. But for centuries change must have been slow. The ceremonies continued their course, year after year; the methods of agriculture met with no revolution; the ancient customs conformed to the grooves that long experience and endless repetition had worn for them.

With the coming of the first continuous white contact, the establishment of an agency, and the opening of a school, a new force had arisen. At first, and for a long time, this had little impact. To be sure, a few young folk learned to speak English. White government set up a reservation and began to issue orders, but the Hopi language continued to be the only one spoken in most homes, and the ways of the whites did not penetrate far. The major characteristics of Hopi life continued as they had been for decades.

With the passage of time the schools were extended, both in number and in the percentage of children that they enlisted. Another generation of young folk—the men and women now in their fifties and sixties — went to school, and the English language came into wider use. Again the wheel turned, and the grandsons and granddaughters of those first school children were learning the manner of speech and the ways of the whites. Now, still another generation has been added.

Thus today, the original Hopi stock, influenced only in part and often only indirectly by the whites, is represented by men and women of eighty or beyond, many of whom speak English. Following them come the other generations, who, in successive steps are gradually becoming more and more influenced by the whites. Now, schoolchildren sometimes travel one hundred miles or more in a bus to a basketball game.

It must not be assumed that revolutionary change has been going on throughout the period since the first school opened its doors. For many years change was slow and relatively minor in scope. The influence of Hopi customs, so long fixed and deeply ingrained in thought and belief, was strong. It remains a potent force to this day. The fact that the Hopis do not, as a rule, intermarry with other races has kept the stock unaltered and therefore strongly inclined toward the traditional ways and views. The geographical isolation of the Hopis has given them a physical barrier. Whites flock to Snake Dances, but see little else, and roads, until recently, have been whimsical in bad weather.

Seemingly, in the last few years, a different change has begun. The World Wars and the returning veterans have contributed to it. Road building, especially the advent of a hard-surface through road, has begun to play a part. A new emphasis on earnings expressed in money is making itself felt. The relocation of a considerable number of families on irrigated land near the Colorado River—a federal government project—and the accounts which they send back of crop yields and cash returns raise questions. The vision of extensive funds through negotiations with the federal government for settlement of land claims, focuses attention on monetary economics; possible oil deposits do the same. Perhaps most potent of all, the advent of government welfare and pension checks affects thinking.

Tribal government has still to prove that it can operate with constructive and certain success. Indians and whites, alike, hope that it can succeed. In these times of complicated human relationships, problems which are as wide as the Hopi culture and as extensive as the land which they occupy require joint efforts and decision. Based, as it is, on our accustomed democratic procedure, the existing form of tribal organization runs headon into the ancient autonomy of the Hopi village. There are many who say that we ourselves, with no such obstacle to overcome, have not yet wholly succeeded.

Some white observers believe that the whole idea of a reservation, under federal supervision, should be abandoned, that the Indian should be "freed" to take his place among the rest of our population. Aside from the matter of schools and their support, roads and their maintenance, hospital care, and all the other essentials now provided, there is another and a deeper question to be answered. A Hopi friend of mine, whose mind is broad and keen, speaks of it this way:

"There are individual Indians who are fully capable of holding their own in the white civilization. There are more of them than there used to be and the number is increasing. But there are many more who are not yet ready. To throw them all into unguided contact with the whites would be disastrous and unfair.

"The white civilization is too complicated. It moves too fast. It involves many things which are foreign to Indian experience and are beyond his judgment. An Indian is not accustomed to dealing with large sums of money or their wise expenditure. He would squander such money because he has had no experience in its management. He is not ready for democratic government. He does not accept the decision of a majority and adopt it as his own. All his life he has believed that a man is entitled to form his own judgment and to map his own course. That has always been the rule as he has been taught. If a man desires something, everyone else lets him have his own way. If he refuses to agree to something, he is not to be forced. If he does something which turns out well, he is entitled to the benefit, and if it turns out wrong, he has to put up with the results. But nobody interferes, either way.

"It will take a long time to change this way of thinking. New generations will have to be raised which have been taught to look at things as the white man looks at them. They will have to think in the white man's language and adopt his point of view. When that has come about, when an Indian tribe has learned to manage its affairs successfully in the way which white civilization has adopted, it will be time to let the Indian take his place in white society."

Meanwhile the oldest generation of Hopis, the men and women who are now eighty years old or more, stand as living representatives of an ancient way of life. They have not been greatly touched by the transition that has begun. When they are gone, there will be no others, I think, who are quite the same.

PRONUNCIATION

PERSONS APPEARING IN THE TEXT

Ba′toti	Baah′-toh-tee	"Water all over"
Cho′ro	Choh′-roh	"Bluebird"
Du′wa	Dü′-wah	"Sand"
Ho′ko	Hoh′-koh	"Juniper"
Hova′kpi	Hoh-vah′-kpee	"Sand sagebrush"
Hona′psi	Hoh-nah′-psee	"Red corn ear"
Hon′hoya	Hohn′-hoy-ah	"Little bear"
Hon′mana	Hohn′-mah-nah	"Bear maiden"
Humi′ta	Hoo-mee′-tah	"Shelled corn"
Ka′chi	Kah′-chee	"Foxglove"
Kel′hoya	Kell′-hoy-ah	"Little sparrow hawk"
Ko′ko	Kŭh′-kŭh	"Burrowing owl"
Kwa′ni	Kwah-′nee	"Mescal"
Kwa′taka	Kwah′-tah-kah	"Eagle man"
Ma′kta	Mah′-ktŭ	"Claw"
Mo′vi	Mōh′-vee	"Yucca root"
Na′qua	Nah′-quah	"Head plume"
Siva′pi	See-vah′-pee	"Rabbit brush"
Ta′bo	Taah′-boh	"Rabbit"
Taku′ri	Tah-koo′-rzee	"Yellow corn"
To′chi	Tōh′ chee	"Moccasin"
Tu′va	Too′vah	"to throw"

The Hopis

CEREMONIES, CHARACTERS, AND PLACES

Au'halani	Aou'-hah-lah-nee
Ba'kabi	Baah'-kah-bee
Chaa'kmonwi	Chaah'-kmong-wee
Ki'sha Ma'na	Kee'-shah-Mah'-nah
Ki'sha Ti'yo	Kee'-shah-Tee'-yoh
La'uwa	Lah'-oo-wah
Masau'u	Mah-sau'-oo
Mishong'novi	Mish-ong'noh-vee
Niman	Nee'mahn
Omau'u	Oh-mau'-oo
Pa'hola	Pah'-hoh-lah
Patki	Pah'-tkee
Shungo'pavi	Shun-gmoh'-pah-vee
Sicho'movi	Tsee-cho'moh-vee
Soya'la	Soy-ah'-lah
Soya'luna	Soy-ah'-loo-nya
Tawa A'hoyi	Tah'-wah-Ah'-hoi-ee
Tawa'pa	Tah-wah'-pah
Walpi	Wahl'-pee
Wu'wuchim	Woo'-woo-chim

COMMON WORDS

apa'bi	ah-pah'-bee
a'sa	aah'-sah
bam'navi	bahm'-nah-vee
cha'mya	chah'-meeah
eskwa'li	ers-kwah'-lee
hati'quo	hah-tee'-quoh
ha'yoma	hah'-yoh-mah

262

he′yta	hĕ′-eetah
hi′sha a	hee′-shah-ah
hi′shat	hee′-shaht
hohoi′si	hoh-hoy′-see
hova′kpi	hoh-vah′-kpee
humi′ta	hoo-mee′-tah
Ie′se e	Ee-ĕ′-sĕ-ĕ
ikwa′chi	ee-kwah′-chee
i′na a	ee′-nah-ah
i′ngu u	ee′-ngoo-oo
ish′pi	ish′-pee
kalo′loma	kah-loh′-loh-mah
kape′te	kah-pĕ′-tĕ
ka′te	kah′-tĕ
kawi′tnga	kah-wee′-tngah
keve′fsi	kĕ-vĕ′-fsee
ki′hu	kee′-hoo
ki′ma	kee′-mah
kiva	kee′-vah
kucha′nuptu	koo-chah′-noop-too
kutu′ki	koo-too′-kee
ku′yi	koo′-yee
kuyiva′to	koo-yee-vah′-toh
kwa′chi	kwah′-chee
kwa′kwai′	kwah′-kweye′
kwa′ngwa	kwah′-ngwah
kwapi′bhu	kwah-pee′-boo
kwu ma′	kwü-mah′
lo′loma	loh′-loh-mah
ma′ka	mah′-kah
ma′na	mah′-nah

ma´no	mah´-noh
man´si	mahn´-see
ma´si	mah´-see
masi´phi	mah-see´-pee
ma´spa	mah´-spah
mo´hu	moh´-hoo
mo´ri	moh´-ree
mo´vi	mōh-vee
muz´i	moo´-zree
na´chi	nah´-chee
na´kwachim	naah´-kwah-chim
nana´kofsi	nah-nah´-koh-fsee
nana´kwachim	nah-nah´-kwah-chim
na´shabi	nah´-shah-bee
oe´nga	öe´ngah
ove´e	oh-vě´-ě
o´wa	oh´wah
owa´si	oh-wah´-see
pa´chua	pah´-choo-ah
paho	pah´-hoh
paho´ki	pah-hoh´-kee
pa´hu	pah´-hü
pa´ki	pah´-kee
paki´to	pah-kee´-toh
pa´kwa	pah´-kwah
pa la´	pah-lah´
pa´ngna	pah´-ngah
pa´pu	paah´-poo
pa´tki	pah´-tkee
pa´tni	pah´-tnee
patu´bha	pah-too´-bhah

pavai′o	pah-vai′-oh
pava′tiya	pah-vah′-tee-yah
pa′vunuvi	pah′-voo-noo-vee
pawi′ki	pah-wee′-kee
Pe′o ia′ a	Pĕ′-oh-ee-ah′-ah
pe′te	pĕ′tĕ
Pi′i	Pee′-ee
pi′kalup kuto′ki	pee′-kah-lup koo-toh′-kee
pi′kami	pee′-kah-mee
pika′viki	pee-kah′-vee-kee
pika′vik pa′nga	pee-kah′-vik pah′-ngah
piki	pee′-kee
pi′kya	pee′-keeah
pi′va	peee′vah
sa′hu	saah′-hoo
sa kwa′	sah-kwah′
sa′mi	sah′-mee
samo′a	sah-moh′-ah
si′hu	see′-hoo
sikya′nuptu	see-keeah′-noop-too
sipa′la	see-pah′-lah
si′ta	seee′-tah
siva′pi	see-vah′-pee
si′wi	see′-wee
so′nwaiyo	soh′-nweye-yoh
su′ovi	soo′-oh-vee
suvi′fsi	soo-vĭ′-fsee
ta′bki	tah′-bkee
ta′bo	taah′-boh
ta′la	tah′-lah
tala′si	tah-lah′see

265

The Hopis

tala′vaiyi	tah-lah′-veye-yee
ta′shubi	tah′-shoo-bee
ta′wa	tah′-wah
tawa′kchi	tah-wah′-kchee
ta′waki	tah′-wah-kee
tawa′si	tah-wah′-see
tawa yama	tah′-wah yah′-mah
te′va	tĕ′-vah
tih	tĭ
tipo′si	tee-poh′-see
Tokil′na sha′ptu	Toh-keel′-nah shah′-ptu
tu i′tsma	too-ee′-tsmah
tu′mi	too′-mee
tumoi′viki	too-moi′-vee-kee
tu′moki	too′-moh-kee
tu′oyi	too′-oh-yee
tu′pebu	too′-pĕ-boo
tu u′nava	too-oo′-nah-vah
tuve′e	too-vĕ′-ĕ
Um haka′mi	Oom hahkah′-mee
Um′pu′niman	Oom′-poo′-nee′-man
wi′kwapi	weee′-kwah-pee
wi′wa	weee′-wah
ya′wma	yah′-wmah
ye′se	yay′-say

PHOTOGRAPHIC DATA

All of the portraits in this book were made on 35 mm. Kodachrome film, daylight type. Three were made outdoors, with synchronized, fill-in flash. The rest were made indoors with synchronized flash as the sole source of light, using outdoor Kodachrome, which is balanced for a color temperature of 6,000K, and blue flash-bulbs, Sylvania 25B, which emit light of approximately the same temperature.

The camera was a Leica. The lens was 90 mm., either an Elmar or a Kilar, the latter mounted in a Kilfitt reflex housing. In all portraits indoors, the camera was on a tripod and the subject was seated. The distance—camera to subject—varied from five to six feet. Synchronization was set to permit approximately full value of the flash bulb. The stop used varied from F5.6 to F9, depending on the distance, camera to subject, and the reflectance characteristics of the room in which the picture was made.

Usually the subject was seated several feet from a rear wall or corner of the room, and the background, therefore, was not much illuminated by the flash, which was adjacent to the camera. In some cases, the background was lighted by a second synchronized flash.